Early Modern Europe

Oxford Paperbacks University Series
include many books previously published in
the Home University Library, founded in 1911

SIR GEORGE CLARK

Early Modern Europe
from about 1450 to about 1720

Second Edition

OXFORD UNIVERSITY PRESS

London *Oxford* *New York*

Oxford University Press
LONDON OXFORD NEW YORK
GLASGOW TORONTO MELBOURNE WELLINGTON
CAPE TOWN SALISBURY IBADAN NAIROBI DAR ES SALAAM LUSAKA ADDIS ABABA
BOMBAY CALCUTTA MADRAS KARACHI LAHORE DACCA
KUALA LUMPUR SINGAPORE HONG KONG TOKYO

First published in The European Inheritance *1954*
Republished in the Home University Library *1957*
Second edition first published as an Oxford University Press Paperback 1966
and reprinted 1970

REPRINTED LITHOGRAPHICALLY IN GREAT BRITAIN
AT THE UNIVERSITY PRESS, OXFORD
BY VIVIAN RIDLER, PRINTER TO THE UNIVERSITY

Contents

A map of Europe showing boundaries of about the year 1500 appears on pp. 8–9.

Preface

THIS BOOK WAS originally the fourth section of a work by various authors, running from prehistoric times to the present, which was published in 1954 under the title of *The European Inheritance*. It is now reprinted with no change other than minor corrections. In the format of the present book it has not been possible to include the illustrations, and the descriptions of these have also been omitted. A note on further reading has been added. I have not given a chronological table of the usual kind, because in such a table it is often difficult for the reader to find a date unless he knows it already. Instead of this the Index includes not only page-references but dates for all the important entries and so will serve as a chronological table.

I wish to express my thanks to Sir Ernest Barker and Professor Paul Vaucher for all that I learnt during our happy association as editors of *The European Inheritance*, and to my son, who read my own contribution in typescript and suggested a number of improvements.

Oxford, 20 February 1957 G. N. C.

1
New and Old in the Fifteenth Century

THERE ARE thousands of people who, although they have neither special historical training nor exceptionally keen perceptions, can judge correctly, nine times out of ten, whether a picture or a carving, or any other object of human workmanship that is set before them, did or did not originate in the western or central Europe of the fifteenth century. The civilization of that time and place had a character of its own which can be recognized in the things that have survived from it, and also in its literature and in much of what is known of its history. When, however, we try to describe such characters, we find them surprisingly elusive: it is far easier to recognize them when they are embodied in a particular product than to set out their essence in words. In a brief summary such as this it is impossible to do more than indicate a few salient points.

The first point is that for many generations the peoples had been used to fixed settlements. The main work of clearing the land, of draining it, and of breaking it in for cultivation had been done for them already by former generations. There were still many places where it could be pushed further, but the pioneering stage was over and the nomadic life was almost forgotten. Almost all the land had its owners. There were wandering flockmasters in Spain, drovers and pedlars everywhere, and armies of mercenary soldiers with no fixed abodes; but these, like the gypsies and the wandering scholars, were exceptional people, moving about in the insterstices of a settled world. The population was very meagre by the standards of our time; but when some change in conditions of livelihood caused a movement of migration, it ended not with the colonizing of empty spaces but with absorption into stable communities which could find work and maintenance for new-comers.

The outward aspects of life were much more diversified by contrasts, by local and regional peculiarities, than they are now, because travel and transport were so slow and difficult, and technology was so primitive, that the physical character of each plot of ground dictated, within very narrow limits, what kind of life could be lived upon it. The area of land which could be cultivated as a single unit, the tools which could be used, the crops which could be grown, the ways in which labour could be organized, depended on whether it was mountain or plain, light soil or heavy, in a wet climate or dry, near a navigable coast or river or far away, and not only on these great variations, which still count for much at the present day, but on far smaller physical accidents. There was little possibility of bringing fertilizers or equipment or even seeds and livestock from a distance; there was little choice of markets. Everything had to be done with local materials if possible, and so in most places farming, whether individual or communal, was not specialized but provided all the requirements of a neighbourhood. In many other spheres the same limitations caused a like variety. There were local styles of architecture, based on the available materials, timber or brick, hard stone or soft. In dress, tools, furniture, conveniences of every kind, the craftsmen of each town had their local fashions.

This variety went deep. It extended to the realm of thought, as may be seen from the instance of language. Each district had its dialect, and, although the dialects belonged to greater languages, such as French or Provençal, Low German or High German, not many people read books or needed to talk to anyone who came from more than a day's journey away, so that standards of correctness in speech scarcely existed. The man who lived at a distance of two days' journey was a foreigner. European man was a local animal.

In spite of all this variety there was one civilization. Below the diversities of systems of farming there was a similarity of social foundations. Almost everywhere individual property existed side by side with community rights. Systems of inheritance were found everywhere, and ownership was based on the monogamous family. Women were in a state of dependence, though not in such complete subjection as in the oriental civilizations. The cultivators were free peasants in some places, serfs in others, while there were places in which serfs and freemen worked together in the same economy; but mere chattel-slavery did not prevail anywhere to any serious extent.

Almost everywhere the division of classes in the countryside conformed to some feudal arrangement. There were distinctions of rank, more or less clearly marked by titles and forms of address, more or less strictly transmitted by inheritance. The higher his rank, the greater opportunities a man had of acquiring riches and surrounding himself with servants and possessions; but the degrees of rank were connected with differences of functions. Justice and the advisory and administrative work of government were largely in the hands of an upper stratum, who were rural landowners and had a military tradition.

The towns had grown up through manufactures and trade. There were many of them, but they were still very small. Paris had possibly 200,000 inhabitants; but most of the famous trading cities, such as Venice and London, were not half that size, while the market towns were proportionately smaller. The merchants and shopkeepers, apprentices and journeymen of the towns did not fit into the class distinctions of the countryside. They had their own forms of organization. One of the distinctive features of European life was the number and vigour of the associations in which the townsmen combined together for economic, social, or religious purposes. According to the balance of strength between rural and urban elements, the towns were subject to the feudal lords in some places, in others independent of them, and in yet others, especially in Italy, they had overcome the country nobility, who now lived as citizens within their walls. But in the towns the fundamentals of the family and of inheritance were the same as in the country. In both alike the leading families formed aristocracies, that is bodies of men who had a claim to hold office not solely by reason of ability or by election or appointment, but by their inherited status. Their common life, their sense of ease and equality among themselves, and of superiority over those with whom they did not inter-marry or share their opportunities, gave them habits of freedom. Many of them had ideals of courage, endurance, loyalty, consideration for women; at their best they recognized that service earned a right to protection, that weakness and inexperience ought not to be exploited, that it was wrong to ask another to run a risk which they would not run themselves. They also showed a harder side when they stood together in order to divide and keep down those who were less fortunate. But there were free men among these 'inferiors' also. There were some among the burghers and the peasants whose status was independent of any man's caprice or favour. Each station and calling had its own standards of conduct, its own wisdom, and its own lapses from them.

Besides all this underlying uniformity there were lines of communication which bound this civilization together and sent impulses through it from end to end. Distance and remoteness impeded intercourse to a degree that we can scarcely imagine nowadays, and yet the paradox is true that the conditions of the time were more favourable to 'internationalism' and to mutual understanding between men from different countries than they are now. We often speak of a medieval 'internationalism' of which the most obvious expressions were the Catholic Church and the use of Latin by the educated classes, and we speak of it as if it resulted from the good dispositions of medieval men, and as if its disappearance was not merely a calamity but somehow reprehensible. This internationalism was, however, in another sense a symptom of weakness in civilization and not of strength. For the very reason that population was scanty, there were altogether very few men who pursued any of the more civilized and civilizing avocations. If these were to reach any high standard, indeed if they were to survive the dangers which beset them in a hostile or unconvinced society, their practitioners must not be solitary, but must to some degree draw together to share their knowledge and stand up for their common interests. Since they could not find enough of their own kind close about them to make such a community as they needed, they formed links with men like themselves in other places. We shall look in a moment from another point of view at the Church, in which the clergy of all Europe were organized for mutual support. We shall look at the universities; but for the present it will be best to take as an illustration one faculty of the universities, that of law, the next in seniority after theology, which stood first. Jurists in the universities were carrying on a great common enterprise of research and teaching. They were improving and transmitting an intellectual inheritance, of which the core was Roman law. Its study was very much alive, and it was proving itself increasingly useful in many countries, in spite of great differences of legal institutions and traditions. Law in general, and Roman law especially, formed an intellectual bond among the innumerable lawyers who practised in the courts or worked as officials for kings or lords or municipalities. The legal faculties of the universities communicated with one another. The lawyers had other, less visible, bonds, and so, although they had no single organization like the Church, they already formed a coherent profession over the whole area which that Church covered, a body which, as the price of its support, exacted from its members some degree of competent knowledge and conformity to a standard of professional honour.

Unity of this second kind, belonging not to the social foundations but to the superstructure of civilization, was transmitted mainly by definite routes. One town was linked with the next by a navigable river or coast, or by a road. The roads over a large part of Europe were chiefly the remains of the great system of military and administrative roads which the Romans had left behind them. They had fallen into disrepair because there was no longer a centralized empire that depended on them; but they still served the needs of the time, and they were sufficiently provided with inns and the other requirements of travellers. The influence of an artistic style or an idea may sometimes be traced along these routes. Building-stone was carried by water, and the map of local styles is often a network of irregular and narrow lines radiating along the rivers from the centres of quarrying. One of the characteristic religious movements of the time was that of the Brethren and Sisters of the Common Life in Germany and the Netherlands. It has been shown that all their houses were established in towns which traded with the annual fairs at Deventer, a few miles from the cloister which the great spiritual writer Thomas à Kempis made famous.

The unifying influence of the Church was the strongest of all, and it operated in many ways. At the highest levels there were conscious movements like that of the Common Life, intentionally propagated through the channels of intercourse; and on the lower level of administrative activity there was no user of these channels to compare with the Church. Its organization was not only far larger than any other of any kind; it was also the oldest, the most experienced, the most regular and methodical in its operation. It preserved orthodoxy in belief by its inquisition; its hierarchy maintained something approaching uniformity of ritual and practice. In practical affairs the whole Church was centralized. Unions and divisions of parishes, dispensations to marry within the prohibited degrees, and innumerable other matters of business were decided in Rome for the whole area which owned the papal supremacy. An ecclesiastical organization so vast and so complex came into daily contact at many points with every kind of authority outside the Church. The landowner might fall out with the parson about tithe or a glebe-farm or a rent-charge; the king had few subjects more powerful than the bishops. In those countries which had been converted during the Dark Ages, ecclesiastics, even though they had no part in the government of towns or villages, sat in the 'estates' or parliaments and often ranked high among the great officers of state. In some places the bishop ruled as a prince; in others, where he had no such rights, his station and abilities might raise him to the highest offices. The clergy as a body were always able to keep some freedom from secular control. Long experience had shown that unmarried priests, even if many of them failed to live up to the ideal of celibacy, could remain free from the entanglements which marriage would have involved in a society founded on the family. They formed therefore, to a far higher degree than the lawyers or the doctors, a profession extending over the whole western world.

All this ecclesiastical structure rose from a common basis as deep and solid as the social groundwork of economic and political life, namely the religious needs of men and women. Apart from exceptions like those of the Jews, who were segregated, or the unconverted heathen of northern Sweden, Roman Catholic Christianity was not only the official religion but also the popular religion. Everyone except the people of the most inaccessible outlying farms could reach a church, and the churches were centres of worship. The parish clergy and the religious orders spread abroad, according to their lights, something of the many-sided devotional, ethical, and artistic inheritance. Every society, association, or institution had its religious observances, and no important transaction took place without the solemnity of an oath or a prayer. It was the Church which laid down and administered the law of marriage, the basis of the family, and so of the whole of society. In these and still other ways civilization was Christian.

No well-informed person supposed that all was well with the Church. There were many complaints of laxity among the clergy, and many writers criticized or satirized them. Europe was full of reformers, authorized or self-appointed, lay or clerical, orthodox or eccentric, local or universal, spiritual or practical, organizers or preachers, worthy or dangerous or merely futile. Some of them had done notable work. The Benedictine Order in the Netherlands and northern Germany had been reformed; high authorities had encouraged some, though not all, of the spontaneous movements of devotion, even when they assumed unaccustomed forms. But these achievements fell far short of what was needed. The Church lay in the shadow of the failure of the movement for reform by a general council; a failure which, after decades of negotiations and preparatory work, had extinguished all hope of a comprehensive and generally agreed reform of head and members. It was recognized that there were abuses in high, even in the highest places, which made it impossible to set matters right below; so that the Church could neither persuade nor compel its members to rise to the requirements of its own universality.

There was a failure of initiative which left the way open to other authorities less universal in their range. The conciliar movements had ended with concordats between the papacy and various kings, of which the general nature was that the central authority of the Church surrendered some of its control and allowed the kings to increase their share in the management of ecclesiastical business. Like most great and long-lasting transferences of authority, this was not merely an arrangement made from above; in some way it satisfied large numbers of the people whom it affected. For a long time national feeling had been growing up in various countries, and it grew most effectively where three factors contributed to it: a growth of vernacular language and literature, a tendency to dissidence or at least to administrative friction in religious matters, and the influence of a vigorous court. All these factors were present in France, and the French monarchy had won a certain degree of autonomy for the Gallican Church; but there were other countries, such as England, in which the gathering force of national consciousness, though perceptible in other ways, had not for a long time past disturbed the balance between the religious and the secular powers. Nowhere, however, were the forces entirely absent which might disturb that balance.

Next to that of the Church the greatest unifying achievement of this civilization was one derived from the Church and still dependent on it, that of organized knowledge and thought. At the middle of the fifteenth century there were more than sixty universities, from Coimbra in Portugal to Prague and Cracow and Buda; others were soon to be founded in north, south, east, and west. These universities were international in many senses. In their reading and teaching, and much of their everyday conversation, the scholars used Latin, the still living language of the Church, and so they were able to travel freely from one university to another, and to find everywhere at least some of the same great books and some of the same habits of mind. All the teaching was watched by ecclesiastical authorities, who had terrible powers of punishment, and this supervision, if it cramped the freedom of speculation, also promoted uniformity and

EUROPE ABOUT

THE YEAR 1500

made it easier for the educated men of different countries to understand one another.

The purpose of the universities was held to be the transmission of true beliefs about the various subjects of study. All the different subjects were held together in an elaborately articulated framework of doctrines. These doctrines had to conform to Christian principles, but there were different schools of philosophers, who disagreed profoundly about logical, metaphysical, and even ethical questions. The range of subjects was fairly wide, though in many of them the amount of actual knowledge was still very small. They included Latin grammar, logic, various literary studies, and not only theology but law, medicine, anatomy, astronomy, the theory of music, physics, and, at an elementary level, some other sciences. In the study of scientific subjects observation played some part, and the testing of hypotheses by experiment was not unknown; but, in general, science was learnt and taught in much the same way as the other subjects. In these there were two main methods. The first was made necessary by the scarcity and high cost of books in the days when they were all written out by hand: it was the exposition of standard textbooks. The second method was discussion. This was carried on in various ways, especially in formal disputations conducted according to set rules. It too was natural in communities of men and boys with few books but with many opportunities for meeting together. These two methods of teaching fostered certain special qualities of mind. Learning and acuteness were highly respected; a good memory, readiness in debate, and skill in constructing systematic arguments were the powers which brought reputation.

For a variety of reasons, some of which we shall notice later, the region in which thought was most active and original, both in the universities and outside them, was the study of classical antiquity. The Greek and Latin classics had always formed an inexhaustible reservoir of thought and imagination. Some of their writers, such as Virgil, were specially esteemed because they were believed to have had a place in the preparation for Christianity; others, such as Aristotle, because Christian philosophers had built on their foundations. But, side by side with these allies of the Christian tradition, there were others who were absolute strangers to it. There were materialists, sceptics, immoralists, and mockers. No censorship concealed them from those who were learned enough to read them; and the scribes of the monasteries and the university towns faithfully transmitted everything in them, even if it was atheistic or obscene. For a long time past the study of this inherited literature had been growing deeper, more comprehensive, and more exact. Forgotten Latin books had been rediscovered; Italian and other scholars had learnt Greek and had begun to collect Greek manuscripts. In 1450 Pope Nicholas V, a friend to these studies, founded the Vatican Library, and by that time there were many active workers both in Italy and beyond the Alps who were investigating not only the languages and literary methods of the Greeks and Romans but also their antiquities in general.

Educated men were coming to believe that ancient literature could teach much-needed lessons in many practical matters. In philosophy and law, and in anatomy and other sciences, indeed, Europe had already been learning from these masters for two centuries, and the only great change now was that the Greek writers were read in their original language, and in this, and other ways were better understood. But the field in which the classics seemed to offer a new revelation was widening, and it continued to expand for more than a century longer, until it included all the arts of government and war and many branches of technology. At this time the fine arts were brought into it in Italy, and there followed the greatest breach in the continuity of artistic tradition in Europe since the fall of Rome. Before this change architecture, sculpture, and painting, with their minor accompaniments such as jewellery and embroidery, were very rich, mature, and varied, providing outward decoration for every phase of social life, expressing many moods, from the heights of mystical religion to the quiet levels of family affection. Whenever there was a respite from the toil of supplying immediate necessities, the craftsman or the needlewoman set to work. There was no clear line between popular and aristocratic art, nor did any distaste for incongruity keep the refined and the delicate apart from the coarse and the grotesque. There had been schools of realistic painting in Italy and outside it for a considerable time, in which the method, though not the purpose, was to paint things and people as they were. Now Italians studied and imitated the classical remains of architecture and sculpture in the buildings and ruins about them. When new fragments were dug up intentionally or by chance they taught new lessons. In 1450 the Florentine Donatello was at work on the equestrian statue of Gattamelata at Padua, more splendid and technically more expert than any work of sculpture that had been made for a thousand years. Fifteen years earlier a writer, Leon Battista Alberti, soaked in the classics and familiar with the paintings of Florence and other north Italian cities, had written a prophetic treatise on painting which drew inspiration —since few ancient paintings survived—from classical sculpture. These two were among the leaders of a great movement of change which brought new skill and new ideals.

This movement of change was in part a revival of classical forms. In architecture the new men imitated Roman buildings so successfully that few people can see any essential difference between the models and the copies. They conceived a building as one whole, and threw away the old traditions of aisle beyond aisle, of pointed arch and crocketed gable, to build flat entablatures and low pediments above their Ionic or Corinthian pillars. In other arts they had not enough of the antique to make a new creative art merely by following the old; they took over this and that, but their antiquarian knowledge was confused and limited, and they did not retreat from the fields of artistic expression which had been opened up in the Christian centuries. They found a new sense of harmony and proportion, of simplicity and directness. They preferred ornaments in low relief to the deep shadows and sharp angles of Gothic carving; but they retained many of the traditional habits of hand and eye in form and colour, so that their revival was not merely learned but was able to live and create.

In their innovations there was a strong intellectual element. In architecture they calculated stresses and measured proportions. In painting they set themselves the scientific problem of representing material objects in relief like the relief of sculpture, straining to see them as they knew them to be in their measurable nature. Thus the higher forms of art began to draw away from popular craftsmanship, and began to be comparatively 'abstract', that is specialized, distinguishing ornament from structure. This intellectual tendency was intimately connected with the classical studies of the scholars. These scholars were not merely discovering what had happened in the past; they stood for intellectual honesty in the search for truth, and they were often critical and sometimes sceptical of the doctrines that were generally received. They began to form 'academies', voluntary societies of courtiers and scholars, who exchanged ideas and literary productions, in a freedom altogether unlike the regulated intercourse of the universities. They felt that they were breaking away from the immediate past and resuming an interrupted continuity with the ancient world. In 1483 Flavio Biondo, a careful student of the monuments of ancient Rome, blocked out the main lines of the history of the world from A.D. 410 to A.D. 1410, as a period different from the preceding and the following ages. He was not the first inventor of this notion. Early in the fifteenth century the great German thinker and ecclesiastic Nicholas of Cues had already referred to this period as the *media tempestas*, the Middle Age.

So far only a few exceptional men were conscious of this transition, but as time went on awareness of it spread, partly for reasons which we shall notice later, until it came to be generally believed that there had been great changes in or soon after the late fifteenth century in all the mutable parts of human nature. A great historian completed the idea by inventing the name 'the Renaissance', the rebirth, under which he tried to group together, as aspects of the revival of antiquity, all the revolutionary changes of those days, not only those which we have mentioned, but also others to which we have still to come. This idea, like the idea of the Middle Ages, did good service, if only in reminding historians how every department of human life is influenced by every other; but it also did harm by leading to fanciful comparisons between the naïve, superstitious men of the ages of faith, whose universe seemed to them familiar and friendly, or at least accessible to conciliation by means of the Church; and the men of the Renaissance, fearless and free, asserting the rights of the individual, pouring out a defiant literature of which Man was the hero, or substituting the cold certainties of science for the comforts of religion. Such interpretations of history try to compress into a phrase and discern in a short stretch of years changes which are never alike in any two men, which are never complete in any one man, which draw their sinuous course through many generations. Continuities are never wholly broken. Many medieval habits and beliefs and institutions persisted until much later; some of them survive, but little altered, in our own time. The Renaissance was gathering force in the twelfth century, and it is still being continued by archaeologists, by grammarians, by artists, and by thinkers.

There is, however, another good reason for taking the middle of the fifteenth century as the beginning of a new age in western civilization. Except in one direction, the importance of which was not yet widely understood, and to which we shall pay attention in later chapters, the west was as good as cut off from the outer world. This one direction was the farthest south-west, where the Spanish kingdoms were on the brink of a new greatness of their own and whence the Portuguese were making their explorations in Africa. Portugal, the first in time of the seafaring states of the Atlantic coast, had a virtual monopoly of trade with West Africa and the Atlantic islands, and this trade brought in not only sugar, gold, ivory, pepper, and other cargoes, but also experience and ideas which in due course were destined to work revolutions. But these still lay in the future. The explorers were not yet in contact with any foreign civilization worth the name; as yet they had encountered only barbarous tribes. Western Christendom had learnt precious lessons in former centuries from one civilization outside its own borders, namely from Islam. Directly, or through Jewish mediation, western scholars were still acquiring something from Arabic learning and science, but little of importance that was new came from these sources now. A few missionaries and an occasional shipload of pilgrims to the Holy Places penetrated into the Islamic world; with the Christians outside Europe there was practically no contact. No other part of the world depended on Europe for its necessaries or its luxuries, and Europe did not derive its necessities from any other part of the world. Few Asiatic and African ships were to be seen in European ports, and the Italian traders, who brought gums and silks and spices from the ports of the Levant, supplied for the most part only the demands of luxury and display. Even in commerce Latin Christendom almost formed a closed world of its own. This isolation helps to explain the intensity of the preoccupation of the west with its own classical past.

Not only was western civilization isolated; there was a great and evident danger that Islam, which held southern Spain, all the North African shore and the Middle East, might overrun central and western Europe as well. The religion of Mahomet is the nearest to Christianity of all the major religions, so near that no Muslim people has ever become Christian and no Christian people has ever become Muslim; but in relation to their social setting the two religions were utterly unlike. The two institutions of polygamy and slavery made the ethical development of Islam differ from that of Christianity, while, on the other hand, they gave it an advantage in making converts. Arabic, the language of the Koran, which had never been translated by Muslims into any other, was the language not only of learning but of commerce; there was no priesthood and no distinction between religious and secular law, so that the merchant was a missionary, as effective in winning proselytes as a priest or a conqueror. To primitive peoples in Asia and Africa Islam brought literacy and the civilizing influence of the belief in one God. The Muslims held the simplest possible views of political authority. They recognized no nobility and no distinctions of rank: the authority of rulers was unlimited in both the religious and the secular spheres.

They offered complete equality to all who accepted Islam; and even those, Christians, Jews, or heathens, who refused to change their religious allegiance were allowed to live and were not denied employment. These infidels were indeed subjected to capricious and sometimes cruel exactions and oppressions; but the advantages offered by Islam even to these classes of its subjects had helped it to spread, as it was still spreading, over a great part of the world. Pilgrims assembled every year in Mecca from southern Spain, from Nigeria, from Java, and from Turkistan. Over the world as a whole the Muslims far outnumbered the Christians. They were indeed divided by religious schisms and political frontiers; but the dynasty which faced Christendom in the east, that of the Ottoman Turks, was a formidable military power. More than a century before, a Byzantine emperor had called in its aid in a civil war, and so had given it a foothold in Europe. Ever since that time it had pushed its frontiers forward, step by step.

Half-way through the fifteenth century the Turks held all western and northern Asia Minor, and in Europe all Bulgaria, Thessaly, and Thrace except Constantinople and a mere patch of land about it. Virtually nothing was left to the eastern emperors except their capital, and this was cut off from the possibility of Christian help by sea or land. One Turkish army had been repelled from its walls a generation earlier, but in 1453 another appeared before them with the most powerful train of siege-artillery that had ever been assembled. The emperor made convulsive efforts to summon help. He offered even the supreme price of ecclesiastical conformity with Rome, but it was too late. The city was stormed and sacked. Under a pile of corpses someone saw eagles embroidered in gold on a pair of shoes, and so identified the body of the last direct successor of Constantine and Augustus.

This was the end of what had once been the most imposing of all Christian states. It gave the Turks the most populous city of Europe, and it made the patriarch of the east, the head of Orthodox Christianity, a subject of the sultan. It did not give great additional resources to the conquerors, and, from the strategic point of view, it merely removed an obstacle; but its moral significance was immense. It led to no answering blow. In the west there was indignant and vociferous emotion, but it was out of the question to organize common military action. There was no crusade.

It was from the south-east that western civilization was threatened; farther to the north its eastern boundary was neither dangerous nor abrupt. The endless plains between the Black Sea and the Baltic were sparsely populated by peoples whose life was relatively self-contained. They imported manufactured goods from the west, especially textiles, metals, and munitions, exchanging them for primary products, the furs and wax of the forests, or corn, flax, and hemp from the cultivated lands. North of the Carpathians most of the inhabitants spoke Slavonic languages. This more northerly region was unlike any other in the world, because there two Christian civilizations had advanced across an intervening belt of heathendom and met. Poland was a fully western country, with the Roman Church, an educated class using the Latin language, universities, and Gothic art. Its kings, however, also held, in loose personal union with it, Lithuania. These two states had combined in successfully resisting the strong power of the Teutonic knights, a crusading military order which had become a territorial power and pressed southwards from its bases on the Baltic. Lithuania had become Christian centuries later than Poland, and its Christianity had come from the south-east; it followed the Orthodox rite, and its ritual language was Church Slavonic. In this, Lithuania was like the lands farther to the east, and in its ways of life it had little in common with Poland. It had no university; western ideas and practices were only slowly permeating it, and although politically joined to the west, economically and socially it had more in common with the east.

This eastern region was divided by vague and fluctuating frontiers, amongst which was one state stronger than the rest, the Russian state called Muscovy from its capital Moscow. There had recently been an ecclesiastical event in Moscow which was a sign of the times. Earlier in the century the Council of Florence had unsuccessfully attempted to reunite the Roman and Orthodox Churches. The Roman Catholics virtually refused to make any concessions to the Orthodox; but there remained a chance that the east, or parts of it, would so far admit western influences as to accept the decrees of the council. A metropolitan bishop of Moscow ventured on this step, but he was deposed. From that time his successors were always Russians, and they were no longer appointed by the patriarch in Constantinople. When Constantinople fell Moscow became the most important independent centre of the eastern Church, and it largely ceased to draw intellectual nourishment from the Greek-speaking world. It may almost be said that Muscovy remained a colonial country but no longer had a metropolis to look to. The grand dukes who reigned there had borrowed some of their methods of government from the warlike Tartar nomads to the east, on whose behalf they still collected tribute from their subjects, but in ceremonial and in the religious conception of monarchy their models were the Christian eastern emperors. Their state, unlike those of the west, had claims over the subject which were limited only by custom. The illiterate population enjoyed little personal or economic security; social life, with extreme contrasts of domination and servility, was completely strange to the few western visitors. Dress, the treatment of women, household furniture, and the ubiquitous eikons before which the people prayed, were all alien. There were no universities; there was no naturalistic art in painting or letters. Yet the Russians were neither Asiatic nor barbarians. They were civilized men, aware of their ethical difference from their Muslim neighbours to the south and their heathen neighbours to the east, and as consciously Christian as anyone in the west. Not only some of their monks and married priests but some of their laymen explored the recesses of spiritual life. But their theologians had not passed through the intellectual discipline of scholasticism; their languages and practices almost isolated them from any exchanges with western thought, so that on this side too the west was communicating nothing and learning nothing from outside.

2
The European State-System

IN MATTERS OF GOVERNMENT there was as much variety as in everything else. There were indeed limits to this variety. No state had two kings like ancient Sparta; no republic had kings as its vassals like ancient Rome. The prevailing types of kingship and lordship had come down from the barbarian conquerors of the ancient world, but institutions had grown up independently in many separate regions, and so had grown up differently. Sometimes a successful device was copied by one state from another; but there was no compelling reason for uniformity.

No clear line distinguished political from economic, especially agrarian, institutions. All property carried with it other rights and duties besides its merely economic rights and duties: the landowner was not merely entitled to the crops from his demesne and the rents or labour-services of tenants; he was, for some purposes, their judge, or their military leader and their representative, even perhaps an elected representative. The burgher not only had the right to keep shop in the town; he took his turn at watch and ward; he could be elected an alderman or mayor and so sit in a court of law. Conversely government was commingled with ownership and there were not yet any supreme authorities which were charged with the duties of legislation, administration, and justice and with these alone. A king's realm was his estate. It might be elective, or it might descend by heredity and be combined with others by marriage, like any other feudal estate. The king had his rights over it, but his subjects as tenants had their rights too, not only in relation to their equals and inferiors, but in relation to their superiors and to the king himself. He had other estates besides his kingdom, and some of them he might hold of other kings. Europe was not divided up into exclusive sovereignties, but covered by overlapping and constantly shifting lordships. The kings, like all other owners, whether feudal lords or peasants, were apt to be hungry or greedy for land; either they added to their dominions or they lost them to stronger and more ambitious neighbours. So dynastic policy, especially in the matter of marriages and hereditary claims, played a great part in their fortunes; and, as it was a rough world, with a headstrong military class, there was constant fighting, both on a small scale between neighbouring owners and on a large scale between neighbouring kings.

Since political authority was proprietary its boundaries were very loosely related to the communities over which it was exercised. It was exceptional for a kingdom to lie all in a piece with clearly marked limits. Detached outlying provinces and islands of foreign territory within the realm were common. The subjects of a king did not usually consist of one national community. The only western kings in whose dominions only one language was spoken seem to have been those of Portugal, and even to this there were some trifling exceptions. At the same time, as with all landed properties in all times, there was a tendency to adjust their boundaries to those of real economic or geographical or social units. It suited the ambitious man better to round off his estate or dominions than to acquire some outlying land that would be harder to manage. It was better for defence to have a definite frontier. It was better for administration, from the subjects' point of view as well as the ruler's, that one man should have the right to all the dues or taxes within a compact dominion than that a number of rivals should send their collectors, with armed escorts, to collect what they could from ill-defined and intermingled areas. It was better for justice and order that criminals should not always have a sanctuary close at hand in some other jurisdiction. So, for a hundred reasons of common sense and general advantage, there was this tendency for kingdoms, like other estates, to become consolidated.

The more consolidated were fitter to survive in the struggle for existence, and they had a better chance of strengthening and rationalizing their organization. Two types of organization were now found almost everywhere side by side. On the one hand was the central administration of the kings and the greater lords. These employed educated and disciplined civil servants, either clerics or laymen, who used such scientific methods as were available, for instance mapping and elementary statistics, for ascertaining the resources of their dominions and laying them out to the best advantage. They hired armies of mercenary troops, more reliable than the feudal levies of knights. They tightened up and systematized the collection of taxes and the administration of justice, often with the aid of the rules of Roman law, which were based on a simple conception of authority and obedience. All this rested ultimately on finance and so on the growth of commercial wealth and of the business class. It had reached a far higher stage of development in the trading republic of Venice than anywhere else. Here an efficient aristocracy directed what was for those days a large international commerce, and ruled over extensive territories in Italy, on the Balkan coast, and in the Greek islands, using systematic statistical information as the groundwork of its policy.

In the simpler and poorer countries, those where town-life was less highly developed, the central authorities could not command such complex machinery. Instead of dealing directly with their individual subjects, they had to receive their information and pass down their decisions through intermediate authorities who were not government servants but who owed their positions to their own rank or power, that is, usually to their positions as landowners or feudal lords. In Poland and Hungary, for instance, central machinery, for lack of a middle class, had made little headway, and the kings could do nothing except through their feudatories. On the other hand the assemblies of 'estates' had spread all over western and central Europe. In order to get the assent of those who would have to pay and obey, kings had always consulted some of their subjects, with more or less formality, and as time had gone on they had found it best to assemble together from time to time not merely the chief men but some of those below them who were coming to have such a mind and status of their own that the feudal magnates could no longer answer for them so satisfactorily as they had once done. The Church had a long experience of elective representative machinery and to some extent this served as an example. Thus most of the kingdoms had general or regional gatherings, more or less rigidly divided up into sections corresponding to the main divisions of the community and reflecting, in their functions and their degree of independence, the position of their members. In most of them there appeared the greater nobles, a select number of the lesser landowners, and representatives of the townsmen. In a good many countries, especially in times of crisis, the estates might venture on opposition to the civil servants, or to the feudal magnates, or to the kings themselves. They might try to enlarge their functions; they might become a factor in the general contest for power.

Although we can generalize to this extent about political conditions, the picture was infinitely confused and irregular and there were exceptions to every rule. In the Holy Roman Empire there were two strata of monarchy, one above the other. The emperor had a very feebly developed central government, with an assembly of estates, called the diet, which came, roughly speaking, from Germany, Bohemia, and parts of the Netherlands. In it there was a house of seven 'electors', powerful princes who elected their emperor; then there was a house representing the less important members of the second stratum, and there were representatives of some of the greater towns. But there were other towns which were subject to the authorities of the second stratum, and these authorities were more than 300 in number, varying in rank and power from the kings of Bohemia through electors, dukes, margraves, and counts to 'free imperial knights' who were no more than small landed proprietors. Each of these, if his dominions were of any size, might have his own assembly of estates. Nominally the empire extended outside Germany, Bohemia and the Low Countries, including northern and central Italy; but here the emperor had few powers left besides that of appointing to vacant fiefs. Here the strongest states were virtually independent principalities like Milan or republics like Venice. Beyond the nominal boundaries of the empire almost all Europe was monarchical. In the west and south the monarchies were hereditary; in Poland, Hungary, Denmark, and Sweden the crowns, like that of the empire itself, were elective.

Christianity stood, as it had always stood in some sense, for an ideal of peace; the word 'peace' sounded in changing contexts through its prayers and observances; but the Church did not command all Christian men never to fight against any of their fellow men. Ecclesiastics taught, as the jurists also taught, that some wars were just, and although they did something towards humanizing and restraining warfare, they did not try to abolish it altogether. Only superior strength could hold back the princes or the feudal lords or aggrieved individuals or even burghers and churchmen from using force to assert what they claimed to be their rights. Every state was organized to fight against anarchy within and against enemies without, and men who looked about them with clear eyes regarded warfare as necessarily bound to recur whenever the conditions were ready for it.

The character of warfare, and the conditions in which it comes about, are always changing, and at this time these changes had effects on the character of civilization. The consolidation of states was not merely a change in their internal structure; it was even more clearly seen in their mutual relations. The conflicts of states and their consolidation furthered one another reciprocally. A state tightened its organization in order to be strong against its rivals, and the strength which it acquired in the contest for power in turn strengthened its government at home. The organs which it developed for conducting foreign policy were specially fitted to act quickly, secretly, and according to unhampered calculations of interest, and so they reinforced the other tendencies which were bringing these qualities forward in social and political organization. The small states of Italy showed perhaps more of these qualities in the middle of the fifteenth century than any others, and it was among them that a new machinery of diplomacy developed. In the Middle Ages the only comprehensive international assemblies were the ecclesiastical councils and the only well-developed system of diplomacy was that which linked the bishops, the religious orders, and other components of the Church with one another and with Rome. The mutual relations of states were carried on by occasional conferences and by intermittent negotiations through heralds, jurists, and ecclesiastics. These ambassadors were distrusted as a ceremonious kind of spies. From about 1448 Florence and Milan found that it suited them in their rivalry with Venice to maintain standing representatives at one another's courts. The Italian states soon multiplied their alliances, undertook greater obligations to one another, for longer periods of time and over a wider geographical area, and this system spread. By the middle of the sixteenth century there was a network of standing diplomacy which covered everything west of Turkey. The sultan received ambassadors but sent none to Christian states.

With the machinery of diplomacy the forms of intercourse developed. There were rules of etiquette. The first manuals of diplomatic practice were compiled. The immunities of ambassadors were defined, such as freedom from arrest and from other kinds of obstruction, for the present without much success: in the sixteenth century they were violated with impunity. The more efficient governments devised intelligence services and received able reports on the affairs of other states. The language of diplomacy was Latin, but as early as 1508 French began to appear in some of the formal documents exchanged in negotiations. In 1504 the first official order of precedence among states was drawn up, a papal list of Christian kings, with a list of ruling dukes which followed it. The body of international law which dealt with larger matters grew more solid and won wider acceptance. The line of the classical writers on international law begins with the Spaniard Francisco de Victoria who was writing in the 1530s. There was no separate diplomatic profession until long after his time—missions were still given to ecclesiastics, jurists, noblemen, soldiers, or other men of position or ability—but there was a diplomatic tradition.

All this was symptomatic of the rise of an actual system of states. From about this time the states of Europe could be classified in war, and in the peaceful combinations which were entered into in anticipation of war, or to prevent it, into three groups. There were great powers; there were satellite allies; and there were neutrals. Much of the history of Europe turned on their action in these capacities or on their movements from one of these classes to another. In building up their strength the great powers availed themselves of support from within the frontiers of other states; they organized and helped their supporters. Thus the internal divisions of states, which had been mainly feudal or local or concerned with the relations between State and Church, now became more involved with international relations, and discontent very often turned into collaboration with the enemies of the state.

The richest, the most populous, and the most highly civilized of all European kingdoms was France. It had perhaps twelve million inhabitants. A great historic achievement had brought a new national consciousness into this feudal society. The expulsion of the English, begun by Joan of Arc, was completed a few weeks after the fall of Constantinople. It left, however, as a sequel a second great national task, that of checking the ambition of the dukes of Burgundy. This branch of the royal house of France had built up a new power on the northern and eastern frontiers of the kingdom. To their original duchy they had added other lands, some of them fiefs of the empire, besides the richest parts of the Netherlands, the greatest western centre of trade and manufacturers. Their court at Bruges was unsurpassed for artistic and ceremonial display and in it worked as able a body of administrators as any in the world. They made conquests and alliances. After a long contest of craft and tenacity their great plans fell to pieces when the duke Charles the Bold was killed in battle in 1477; but the heiress of Charles the Bold still ruled the Netherlands and Franche-Comté, and she took her inheritance in marriage to the Archduke Maximilian, the son of the emperor, who became emperor himself in 1493. France thus became the immediate neighbour of that ever-advancing Austrian house of Habsburg from which the emperors were elected in that age. The Burgundian problem was not ended, or the English problem either, for the English were still in Calais. Their economic interests were closely bound up with those of the Netherlands, and often enough they had found allies there in the Burgundian princes. Towards the end of the fifteenth century the French had a respite from these anxieties, but it was only a respite. In the meantime they were acquiring new lands, and in 1486 the acquisition of Provence gave them an important part of the Mediterranean seaboard.

Along the coast from Provence was Italy, splendid but politically chaotic. Its entire population was perhaps half that of France, but it was divided into a score of little states. The Venetian republic, the most stable, had substantially more than a million inhabitants in its Italian territories. West of it was the duchy of Milan, with nearly a million people, but with less to boast of in government or in the arts. Florence, smaller still, under its Medici rulers, was the most brilliant centre of art and intellect in all Europe. Round these were crowded the duchy of Savoy, with its Alpine passes, the maritime republic of Genoa, the financial and commercial states of Siena and Lucca, and little fighting states ruled by *condottieri* who had troops for hire or, on occasion, for their own ambitious purposes. South of all these the papal dominion, the largest of all ecclesiastical principalities, ill governed and almost disintegrated among the nominally subordinate rulers of its towns, sprawled from sea to sea across the Apennines. The whole of the southern half of the peninsula belonged to the 'Kingdom', Naples, the only kingdom in Italy, sparsely peopled and numbering much less than a million inhabitants. Sicily belonged to the Spanish kingdom of Aragon, but had its own estates and administration.

The royal house of France had feudal claims to the inheritance of both Milan and Naples, not more frivolous than some of the other claims that kings and lords were constantly putting forward as pretexts for aggression. There were exiles who urged the young French King Charles VIII to assert his claims; there were reformers who hoped that he would take up their cause and depose the reigning Pope Alexander VI, the most disreputable of all the popes, the Spanish Borgia. Charles had an army of perhaps 30,000 men, the strongest in Europe. It was not a feudal army. The infantry were foreign mercenaries, largely Swiss, for military service was the chosen export industry of these mountaineers, an industry in which they excelled. The heavy cavalry or *gens-d'armes* were the younger sons of French landowners, first-rate in quality. The artillery and the engineers were the best in the world. In 1494 Charles marched this army into Italy. No one could stop his advance, and by the next year he had settled the affairs of Milan and Florence to his liking and had been crowned king in Naples itself. But the struggle for supremacy in Italy which he began was to last until 1559 and during all that period to dominate the international relations of western Europe.

It was to be expected that even a victorious campaign would give an opportunity for rival powers and that successes in Italy would excite their jealousies. Charles had insured himself against them by a diplomatic preparation for the war. He had provided against any reopening of the Burgundian question by restoring some recently occupied territories to Maximilian, and on his other flank he had conceded a claim of the King of Aragon to two frontier provinces. In making his move into Italy he may indeed have intended to forestall a Spanish intervention there, and it was in no way surprising that Spain should have been one of the powers which drew together defensively when it looked as if Charles would master all Italy. Some of these powers did not matter seriously. Milan was divided by faction; Venice could be bought off with the Apulian ports, and this concession put Venice at odds with the Pope. But the emperor, Maximilian's father, had his rights over the northern Italian states and he had his own ambitions there. And opposition from any of these powers would be dangerous if Spain was behind them.

The history of the Iberian peninsula in the fifteenth century was unlike that of any other part of Europe. For the most part it was barren land much divided by natural barriers, and its population was smaller than that of France, perhaps eight millions in Spain and less than two in Portugal. But while Islam was sweeping forward in the east, the Christian kingdoms of this south-western peninsula were advancing and growing in power. The Portuguese were pushing forward by sea and the Spaniards were driving back the Moors by land. This movement was in some ways comparable with the expulsion of the English from France. It created special types of feudal powers, for instance, great military orders, and fiefs which were almost independent like that of Burgundy. It by no means prevented rivalries between the various Christian kingdoms. In 1462 the kingdom of Castile took a step forward, acquiring Gibraltar and other places, and the right to an annual tribute from the Moors. There was nothing left now of Muslim Spain except the small kingdom of Granada, encircled on the land side from sea to sea by Castile. Castile was feudal and military and had little sea-borne trade. It had more of the crusading spirit than either of its neighbours, Portugal and Aragon, and might look forward to great achievements if it could unite with either of them. Portugal, as we have seen, was the trading and crusading state of the Atlantic. It had been fully independent from the thirteenth century; in the fifteenth it normally enjoyed peace with Castile and an English alliance. It made conquests, and it had a foothold in Morocco and on the west coast of Africa and in the Atlantic islands. On the Mediterranean shore, drawing much of its civilization from France across the Pyrenees, with about a quarter the area of Castile, was Aragon, most of whose inhabitants spoke Catalan, Valencian, and Italian: Aragon looked eastwards. It owned the Balearics, Sardinia, and Sicily. It had close relations with Genoa and Naples.

Almost accidentally dynastic policy brought about a personal union of Castile with Aragon in 1474. It was not converted into an organic constitutional union until long afterwards, and Spain had not moved nearly so far as France in the direction of solid and uniform nationality. In Castile the monarchy had to contend with privileged nobles and municipalities, but the *cortes*, the assembly of estates, were relatively weak; in Aragon they were stronger, and the liberties of the four component parts of the kingdom were firmly rooted. But Ferdinand and Isabella built up a strong central administration of the new professional type, which gradually strengthened its hold over government at the expense of all the other authorities. The 'Catholic kings', as they were called, acquired a unique control over ecclesiastical affairs, an ecclesiastical despotism. The personal union immediately altered the whole political state of the peninsula. The Moors in Granada were foolish enough to refuse to pay their tribute and to seize a frontier fortress. There followed a war of ten years, from 1482 to 1492. Granada was divided by dynastic quarrels. The Castilian fleet cut it off from Africa and blockaded its ports. The Spanish army was mainly feudal, and it was poor in quality; but there was enthusiasm behind it. A new national force, the *hermandad*, was recruited; Switzers were hired and other foreigners volunteered. It was a war of sieges, and the Christian artillery and engineers, some of them foreigners, though crude were effective. Granada surrendered on liberal terms and the last Muslim kingdom in western Europe disappeared. The terms were violated; there were rebellions and punitive expeditions until 1508; but there has never been any revival of Moorish rule.

A new power was coming into existence. At the same time Spain displayed a new mastery in many of the arts of civilization. During the war Queen Isabella started the first modern field-hospital. In the year when it ended one of her subjects presented to her the first grammar of the Castilian language, which was the first grammar of any modern language. New universities were founded. Thought was active; organization, discipline, the assimilation of the newly conquered south moved forward together. The conquest of Granada naturally led to a further advance in the same direction. It was followed immediately by a reconnaissance of North Africa, to which the refugees from Granada had crossed. In 1509 the great minister Cardinal Ximenes accompanied an expedition which captured Oran.

The Spaniards held Oran for 200 years, and they followed up its conquest by taking Tripoli; but their pressure rallied the forces of Islam, and the conquest of Egypt by the Turks enabled them to come to the rescue of Tunis and the newly founded Algiers. In alliance with the Turkish sultan these two states were saved by sea-power, and the Spaniards, from about 1515, were checked by a new maritime resistance, a Holy War at sea. And the Spaniards had never turned their backs on Europe to concentrate their new energies on Africa. The western Mediterranean was a single theatre of trade, of politics and of war, and from the first successes of Charles VIII of France in Italy, Ferdinand and Isabella had been drawn into the Italian struggle.

The price which Charles had paid for their neutrality was high; but they watched every step of his advance with jealous apprehension, and the bribe was not rich enough to make them contemplate with equanimity the sight of a French king in Naples. The French were sometimes powerful and sometimes weak, but no other power took a strong initiative in Italy. The Italian states and the neighbours of Italy grouped themselves in short-lived alliances, chopping and changing as they hoped more from uniting against the French or from sharing in the spoils of French victories. Charles's rule in Naples lasted only from summer to autumn: when Ferdinand, the emperor, the Pope, Milan, and Venice combined against him he had to withdraw. Two years later the emperor and Venice dropped out of the coalition; but the Spaniards and the Neapolitans drove the French forces out of south Italy. A second phase of the French adventure began when Charles's cousin Louis XII succeeded to the throne in 1498. He handed over a further instalment of frontier places to the Duke of Burgundy to keep him neutral, and he had both the Pope and Venice on his side. For a time it looked as if this would lead to a rearrangement of the map of Italy. The French established themselves in Milan and gratified the ambitions of Venice for an improved land-frontier. Caesar Borgia, the ruthless and able son of the Borgia pope, made the papal state into an efficient despotism. Ferdinand of Aragon thought it best to agree to a partition of Naples. But these events did not correspond with the realities of power. Venice lost a sea-battle against the Turks, and had no strength to maintain the new mainland possessions that she had rashly acquired. The Spanish army had been quietly growing in size and efficiency, especially its infantry. When Louis accepted the surrender of Naples from its king, he brought this force down upon him. The Spanish general, Gonsalvo de Cordova, 'the great captain', marched through the kingdom winning battles. The French failed miserably in a double invasion of Spain to the east and to the west across the Pyrenees. Naples was annexed to Aragon in 1504, and the dream of French power in southern Italy was ended.

For the remaining ten years of his life King Louis still counted for something in Italy, but his footing there depended on the vicissitudes of the constantly shifting alliances, and the French showed no greater common sense than the sharp-witted Italians in distinguishing petty immediate gains from solid and permanent interests. Louis tried an offensive alliance with Burgundy, but this time he tendered so great a price in territory that the French states general made a stand for national interests, declaring that the provinces which he offered were inalienable and that the princess whose dowry they were to be must marry Louis's own heir. The last remaining ally was the Pope, the warlike Julius II, and it was Julius who gained from this combination, by turning the French against the Venetians and taking all he needed from the republic. The Emperor Maximilian, who joined in the attack on Venice, failed to win anything. Then the French quarrelled with the Pope. They talked of a council, and a council, hostile to the Pope, did meet at Pisa and afterwards at Milan. Louis had victories, then defeats, then victories again in north Italy. In 1515 he died, and his successor, Francis I, had to face renewed war with Spain. He marched an army over the Alps, won a battle, and broke the power of the Swiss in north Italy. In 1516 there was a settlement. The French claim to Milan was recognized and the Pope restored the disputed border-places to it. The Concordat of Bologna regulated the relations of Church and State in France. This diminished the power and independence of the bishops and handed over much of the control of ecclesiastical affairs to the king and the Pope. As between these two it amounted almost to a grant of independence to the Gallican Church. Thus Francis, like Ferdinand, though to a lesser degree, had added ecclesiastical to his temporal power.

There were indeed ideas in the air which denied the whole way of thinking on which the settlement was founded. Two books which were written in the year 1513 show how fundamental they were.[1] Niccolo Machiavelli, a Florentine official who was an historian, a playwright, and a master of Italian prose, wrote his *Prince*, a handbook of the arts of political success. It admits no place in these arts to justice or mercy, and its hero is Caesar Borgia; but it calls up the vision of an Italy united and free from foreign rule. The other masterpiece of 1513 was the anonymous pamphlet *Julius Exclusus*, a dialogue on the shutting out of the dead Pope Julius from the Heaven which he had not deserved. This denunciation of the worldly and victorious pontiff was an expression of Christian ethics, but there was something revolutionary in it. It was written secretly by Erasmus, a classical and Biblical scholar of the highest celebrity, born in Holland but a restless wanderer over Europe, brought up as a churchman but never satisfied with the life that the Church could offer him. Like Machiavelli's book it was not medieval: it had a directness that derived something from the ancient classics. And in their different ways these two books were signs of fundamental changes in civilization then coming to fruition, to which we must soon turn our attention. Before we do that, however, we must look at eastern Europe and see how its relations with the west were affected by the changes we have already noticed.

Naturally both the intellectual movements and the changes in political organization had their influence in that part of the world. About the middle of the fifteenth century Italian architects went to work in Moscow, where Italian work still stands in the Kremlin. But the fall of Constantinople came at a time when Muscovy was growing stronger. The Tartars of the Golden Horde were weakened by emigrations, and the Prince Ivan III, called the Great (1462–1505), by allying himself with the Khan of the Crimea, played off one set of Tartars against another and freed himself from paying tribute. As the

[1] Machiavelli's *Prince* circulated freely in manuscript during his lifetime but was first printed, with papal sanction, in 1532 after his death; the *Julius Exclusus* was published in 1514 at Cambridge.

Turks advanced in the Black Sea region the western powers turned their eyes in that direction, seeking for allies. The Papacy and Venice arranged a marriage between Ivan and a niece of the last eastern emperor. As late as 1519 a papal legate was in Moscow spinning plans. The Habsburgs also tried to draw Ivan into their system of alliances. In 1486 a Silesian merchant travelled across Lithuania to Moscow and reported to Vienna what he had seen. He was sent back on a diplomatic mission: the Emperor Maximilian offered to invest Ivan as king and to bring him into the European system. Ivan replied that he needed no investiture. He made the startling suggestion of an offensive alliance to gain Hungary for Maximilian and Lithuania for himself. The exchanges of diplomatic missions with the emperor led to no more results than those with the popes. From the point of view of the west Muscovy was a new but an intractable power. From the Russian point of view a western question had arisen, the problem how to take advantage of western technical skill without losing independence. At the same time the west and the Baltic were the most inviting field for using the state's new strength to make conquests. The Turks were strong and there was every reason to trade with them and to maintain friendly relations. Ivan III invaded Finland. The trading republic of Novgorod was the centre of trade with the league of north German cities called the Hanse, and it was a centre of Russian civilization only less important than Muscovy. Ivan turned against it and mastered it. He transferred some of the inhabitants to the south, and terminated the trade of the Hanse. Then he made war on Lithuania, and a few years after his death the Russians took Pskov and Smolensk. In 1518 Ivan's successor, Basil III, in official correspondence with the emperor, used the title of tsar, the Russian form of Caesar. That was as much as to say that there was a second state-system over against that of the west and not to be absorbed into it, but a system consisting of one state. Nevertheless, Russia was not yet a great power like the consolidated states of the west. It could not compare with them in military strength. It was ambitious, but ambitious rather to extend its frontiers than to conquer other states. It did not contemplate adventures at a distance.

No considerations of distance limited the ambitions of the Turks, nor did they feel any doubt of their military superiority to the west. That the west had special skill in certain arts and industries they recognized; but the products could easily be bought. Curiosity about western ways did not lead to imitation. Mahomet II, the conqueror of

Constantinople, sat for his portrait to the Venetian painter Vittorio Carpaccio, whose pictures of St. George and St. Ursula are popular nowadays for the naïve and childlike sentiment that is mistakenly read into them. But he did not westernize his army or his state.

The social organization of the Turkish empire was utterly unlike that of Europe and it was well fitted to turn military victory into lasting conquest. There were no legally recognized distinctions of status or class. The Turks themselves were a minority, but they were not a governing class. Among the officials, who were entirely dependent on the sultan, were Slavs, Greeks, Albanians, Georgians, and some Italians. The Greek Church was as docile to the sultans as it had been to the Byzantine emperors. Many Christians kept their lands or gained promotion by renouncing their faith, but the remainder were contemptuously tolerated. Although there was no industry, and the export trade in Syrian silks and Egyptian spices was in the hands of Europeans, the state had the largest and most regular revenues of any, and it was the only state in Europe with a constant surplus. Taxation was light and diminished as the empire grew, because there was no proportionate increase of the army. The military equipment was inferior to that of the west, but artillery was imported, and though the Turkish artillery was inferior in quality, none of it was needed to preserve internal order and so the whole was available on the frontier. In the same way the technical inferiority of the other troops, who were drawn from relatively backward peoples, was outweighed by their numbers and organization. They were not mercenaries, like those of the west or those of the old eastern empire; they were conscripts, raised by the 'tribute of children' mainly from conquered Christian territories in Europe, especially Serbia and Albania. These janissaries, of whom there were 8,000, could not marry. They were the only standing army of the time, the only army that remained on foot through the winter from one campaign to another. In quality they were inferior to the best western infantry, but their pay was regular, their musters were full; commanders and men spoke one language. They were the nucleus of an army in which the best troops were the numerous light cavalry. This was the period in which infantry was taking the place of cavalry as the decisive arm; but for the present the Turkish land forces as a whole were very nearly invincible. At sea they had no such advantage. They had many ships; but they were badly built and the crews were badly trained.

The Ottoman empire was far more powerful than any European state, and it was growing. Between 1485 and 1559 its area was trebled.

In his reign of thirty years Mahomet II subjugated all the remaining Greek independent states, besides Albania, and all the remaining Slav states in the Balkans except for the region about Montenegro. He took the Genoese possessions in the Crimea and made the Crim Tartars his tributaries. He did indeed fail before Rhodes, and the Venetians held on to a few points on the eastern coast of the Adriatic besides their islands, but at the end of his life he made the formidable advance of establishing his power on the heel of Italy by capturing Otranto. A year later, after Mahomet's death, Otranto was retaken. Islam never again came so near to closing the Adriatic or to overrunning Italy; but farther east its advance was not checked. Moldavia, which had regained its independence in the latter part of the fifteenth century and even set out on a brief career of conquest, was overpowered early in the sixteenth. The defence of the Levant was improved when the Venetian republic accepted the cession of Cyprus from its last queen; but ten years later the Turks defeated the Venetian fleet, and Venice returned to her normally amicable relations.

Europe was preserved only because their European affairs were always less important to the Turks than those in Asia. From 1512 to 1520 the Sultan Selim the Grim made enormous advances there. He took wide provinces from Persia. Turning southwards he conquered Syria and Egypt. These events gave Europe a respite; but they portended danger.

If the western states had been capable of combination they could have taken advantage of the weaknesses of the Turks in armament, in infantry, and at sea; but they were incapable of it. They allowed the Turks to attack them one at a time. The Catholics did not help the Orthodox. The Venetians did not wish to endanger their commerce with the Levant. If they bestirred themselves they were hampered by the jealousies of their Italian neighbours, and by the Austrian Habsburgs who were increasing their territories at the head of the Adriatic. So, in the eighty years after the fall of Constantinople there was nothing resembling an alliance against the Turks. The growth of the western state-system was feeble in comparison with the mounting Turkish danger.

3
Printing

IN THE YEAR after the fall of Constantinople Pope Nicolas V proclaimed an indulgence, a remission of spiritual penalties for their sins, for all who would contribute money to the defence of Cyprus against the Turks. It happens that the announcement of this indulgence is the earliest piece of paper printed from movable type in Europe to which we can assign a definite date. We have no reason to suppose that anyone foresaw the full significance of this new technological contrivance. Certainly Mahomet II, if he ever heard of it, did not infer that the west had new reserves of strength and inventiveness which in time would reverse its relations with the east. Looking back on it now we can see, in spite of many obscurities in our defective records, that the invention of printing, as we commonly call it, was more than a signal that enormous changes were to come. It also proved that the way had already been prepared for them by a number of converging alterations in society.

Something of the same sort had been known in China long before this time, and we cannot be certain whether the Europeans learnt printing directly or indirectly from the Chinese or found it out for themselves. We do not even know exactly when or where it was first practised in Europe, but our ignorance of these matters reinforces the knowledge that the new art was not brought full-grown from outside to a western civilization wholly unprepared for it, as the telephone was brought to nineteenth-century Africa. There had been a series of preparatory stages on the technical side. As early as the thirteenth, or even the twelfth, century designs had been printed on textile fabrics from wood blocks cut in relief. Until the beginning of the fifteenth century writing had to be done on parchment and similar materials made from skins, of which the quantity was necessarily limited and the price comparatively high. From that time, however, there were ample supplies of rag-paper, and these made it possible for book-production and writing in general to expand indefinitely. Block-printing on paper came in: there were woodcut pictures of saints, and playing-cards. Then only a few adaptations of presses and block-making were necessary to perfect the art, and the final steps were taken most likely in Mainz, a rich trading town and a cultivated ecclesiastical capital.

The preparation had been not only on the technical side; it also sprang from changes in men's minds. So far as we can tell, the technical improvements could perfectly well have been made much earlier if anyone had wanted them, and there are two reasons for thinking that in some way a new desire for devices of this kind came into being. First, although most historians now reject the competing claims of places other than Mainz to call the invention their own, there is enough substance in them to prove that it was taken up very quickly in other places, particularly in that great centre of the arts and manufactures, the Netherlands. It may even have been worked out independently in more places than one at about the same time. Secondly, printing was not the only development from the wooden block-engravings. Men were, we may say, experimenting outwards from this in various directions. One was *intaglio* engraving, in which, instead of standing up like the black parts of type or of a woodcut, the engraved line is cut into the wood or metal, and the paper is pressed into it to take the ink. A whole group of methods of engraving are based on this principle, so that before the middle of the fifteenth century artists had at their disposal several methods of reproducing their works exactly in many copies.

This was something new, something which immediately began to change men's ways of seeing and working. There were some engravers who made their own drawings, others who engraved pictures drawn by other men for other purposes. Works of art became familiar which were not unique, or approximately like their originals, as hand-drawn copies may be, but so nearly identical that for ordinary purposes there was no difference. Many people could possess the same picture. That was a very great change, but there were others. By constantly seeing woodcuts and other engravings, people acquired a new habit or power of seeing not in colour but in black and white, which in some ways enriched and in other ways impoverished their mode of seeing. The world of sight and imagination altered. For nearly 400 years—until the beginnings of photography—there was no fresh development to compare with this, but throughout these centuries the modes of seeing continued to change, gaining new delicacies of perception or losing familiar satisfactions. Besides these changes in and from the visual arts there ran even greater and more frequent changes in the nature of reading and writing, and their uses in life, more pregnant because they affected all kinds of men and women in almost everything they did or thought.

No sooner was printing discovered than a great demand for printed books and papers made itself effective throughout all the Latin area. Within a generation there were presses at work in France, Italy, Spain, the Netherlands, England, and Denmark. Before the end of the century Portugal and Sweden had them, and even Montenegro, the Balkan outpost. Books, of course, could be exported to countries where there was no printing; in the sixteenth century a well-organized international book-trade grew up, serving most of the western countries. From the very first there were two kinds of copy for the printers, just as there were two kinds of originals for the engravers. On the one hand the printers made available editions of the books already existing in the world, every sort of books, from the Greek and Latin classics to the most recently popular romances. This task was so enormous that it has not yet been, and probably never will be, completed: there were so many books and documents in manuscript that it was necessary to select the most important, but, as the process went on, fresh claims were always coming forward, either from chance discoveries in old libraries or from the opening up of whole literatures, like those of the east, as the knowledge of languages extended. In both these ways the expansion of the known past in literature has always gone on with endless acceleration. On the other hand—and this is the main reason why the printers have not caught up with the printing of what was already written before printing was invented—they have always had to divide the use of their machinery between this task and the competing task of printing what was being newly written in their time. Along with the old, the first printers also disseminated the new, and very soon there were talented authors who wrote specially for the press. We have seen already that they lived in a time when the new, in literature and thought, was exceptionally different from the old, and exceptionally attractive. By putting it quickly into many people's hands, and by postponing the printing of much that had recently become old-fashioned, the early printers helped to cut off their contemporaries and their successors from the immediately preceding centuries.

Books could now be produced far more quickly, far more cheaply, and in far greater numbers. This was a revolution, a revolution continuing until, in our own time, the new inventions for reproducing sound have ended the age in which the printed word has been the main vehicle for spreading knowledge, information, ideas, and even emotions abroad. Beneath all the events of these centuries there has gone on the change from the first printers, who could put out a few hundred copies of a book in a few weeks, to the modern printers who can make a million copies of a newspaper in a few hours. The world has been filled with these uncountable printed sheets and volumes, large and small, cheap or costly, rare or universally familiar, durable or ephemeral, treasured or neglected, commonplace or exquisitely beautiful. Every one of them has left some result behind it, and the sum of these results is far beyond calculation.

It is easy to see that printing made the spread of literacy much easier; and the power to read and write is an instrument of authority if it belongs to a few, but a stepping-stone to equality if it belongs to many. As the number of readers increased, the influence of writers grew with it. In universities, in public affairs, and among general readers there were more books to be had, and so the more personal influence of the teacher or expositor gave way before the might of the book, of the unseen author. Literary reputations could be made and spread as quickly as ships and horses could carry packages of books. Erasmus had a European reputation, and every book he published was known from one end of the continent to the other as soon as it was ready. Every man who could read or be read to was accessible to persuasions, propaganda, from far and near, perhaps authorized, perhaps directed against established ideas and institutions. Governments and the Church, trying, in accordance with their traditions, to keep their control of men's minds, made rules of censorship and new institutions for enforcing them; but the simple machinery of government which they had at their disposal was often unable to dam the rising streams. From clandestine presses, through secret channels of distribution, writers could still appeal to their readers against the established order. Even when there was no conflict of opinions, the relation of the writer to his public altered. He worked now through the medium of an industry. From the beginning, by co-operating with the business man who owned and organized the printing-shop, an author could earn money which came from his readers and not from any patron or employer. As the industry grew it offered greater rewards, and so greater freedom, though sometimes it offered them on hard terms. The press, a new institution, with its own mixture of good and evil, stood between the writer and the reader.

Perhaps the greatest changes which printing brought with it were not these social changes, but the changes in language and literature themselves. Printed books set the standards of uniformity for languages, and so the multiplicity of dialects began to give way before a few great standard literary languages, centred on the political or academic or trading capitals. All Englishmen came to write the language of London; all Frenchmen that of Paris; most of the Spaniards that of Castile. This took time, and it happened more or less quickly according to circumstances. In Italy Dante had raised the language of Tuscany to primacy long before; but the country was so divided that there was a polished dialect literature in Venice as late as the eighteenth century. Wherever it did emerge the metropolitan language had a binding and inspiring force of its own, and strengthened the national feeling that was already growing.

In literature the changes were subtle, but radical. It was much easier than before to bring together many books in one place, and so masses of information could be assembled quickly, and the apparatus of learning was transformed. Great books of reference, dictionaries, encyclopaedias, histories, and collections of texts, put at the disposal of every student knowledge which once could not have been gathered in a lifetime. Knowledge of the present was deepened, but also complicated and hindered, by an ever-present consciousness of the past. At the same time standards of correctness became more exacting. With so many identical copies of books before them, not varied by the little touches of individuality which scribes and copyists always introduced intentionally or by accident, readers learnt a new strictness in verbal accuracy and grammatical correctness. The individual work of an author was distinguished more sharply from the inherited or borrowed elements. Copyright became a legal fact, while authorship and plagiarism, as literary and ethical conceptions, were more clearly defined. The Renaissance was helped on, not only as an intellectual movement but as a movement in the art of letters as well. The commonest way of enjoying poetry had been to hear it recited; the commonest way of using a book had been to read it aloud. Now there was so much reading that more and more people read silently to themselves, and books came to be written so that they could best be taken in by the eye and not the ear. Prose gained at the expense of verse; sense gained at the expense of sound. Memory lost some of its value. The story that can be followed without a teller has to be told in a special way: the words themselves, without a voice to clothe them in expression, without accent or intonation, must create their own illusion. So printing set new problems for literature, and as skilful writers devised means of solving them, the range of literature increased until it became, for millions of human beings, almost a substitute for thought and imagination. In the beginning of prehistory speech had given the power of communicating experience, of imagining oneself as a different being, in another time or place. Long afterwards writing had made imagination fixed and lasting and able to add one fancy to another beyond the range of memory, far away from the personal present. Printing set the works of imagination, along with those of thought and emotion, still more securely outside the chances of the present time and place.

4

The Reformations

LIKE JUDAISM and Islam, Christianity had always been the religion of a book; it now became something which the world had never seen before, the religion of a printed book. This need not by itself have meant anything except the addition of a quick-firing weapon of precision to the armoury of the Church. In Spain Cardinal Ximenes, who was Grand Inquisitor as well as minister, saw to the production of a magnificent edition of the Bible in Latin, Hebrew, and Greek. But in countries where the Church was in difficulties with heretics who questioned its doctrines, or princes and laymen who encroached on its rights and its possessions, it was a disturbing factor that thousands of readers, even the most ignorant, could now read the Bible for themselves, drawing their own conclusions from its vast and, in many ways, mysterious contents. The authorized text of the western Church was an old and imperfect Latin translation. Within a century of the rise of printing there had been two enormous changes, closely intermingled at every stage. Vernacular translations had been printed in a number of European languages. The best linguistic and critical skill had been applied to the Hebrew and Greek originals, to establish the true text and, inevitably with far less success, its true meaning. Each of these processes was connected with fundamental controversies in which the participants and the audience were more numerous than in any previous discussions of religious and public matters.

We have seen that strong rulers everywhere, particularly in Spain and in France, strengthened themselves in relation to the Church, and that there were many attempts, on a greater or a smaller scale, to press forward, either by a council or otherwise, the lagging movement of reform. Whether the rulers were actuated by cupidity or by a public-spirited desire to support the reformers, the wealth and power of the existing ecclesiastical institutions were equally likely to suffer. Local and limited reforms might have much good in them, but they upset the existing state of possessions. Strong governments or strong bishops could prevent upheavals; but both at its centre and in its outlying parts the Church in the early sixteenth century was threatened by new tendencies, each of which sometimes checked but sometimes assisted the others. First, intellectual and moral innovations were troubling the uniformity of belief and loyalty to the authorities. The scholars, with their enthusiasm for truth and their formidable good sense, questioned much more than the mere wording of sacred texts. An Italian, Lorenzo Valla, exposed the falsity of a famous document (already called in question by Nicholas of Cues and others) by which the Emperor Constantine was supposed to have granted rights of secular rule to the Papacy. He also gave expression to an ethical theory, by no means novel, which may be called utilitarian: right meant no more than useful, in other words the results to individuals were to be its ultimate test. This doctrine, and even his interest in the startling idea that the papacy was the Antichrist predicted in the books of the Bible, did not prevent Valla from holding an office at the papal court until his death. An eminent Aristotelian scholar, Pietro Pomponazzi, preserving his ostensible orthodoxy by a transparent device, argued against the immortality of the soul; but he did not lose his professorial chair in the great university of Padua. This unsettling of the old beliefs made some men more indulgent, and others more censorious and alarmed, when they saw worldliness and laxity among the clergy, from the popes who lived like magnificent princes to the many priests whose housekeepers were their concubines. The lower the clergy sank, the less chance they had of defending their property. Landowners stole the glebe-lands and used their ecclesiastical patronage as a mere part of their wealth. The popes themselves sanctioned many schemes by which the endowments of canonries or monasteries were taken away and given to universities or colleges, which rulers or statesmen founded in the interests of education.

These far-reaching changes were rumbling throughout most of Europe, but the political circumstances of one country brought it about that there they led to a revolution which transformed the whole political and spiritual life of the continent. This country was Germany. The German language was spoken by more people than any other in Europe. The German part of the Holy Roman Empire was more populous than France: it had somewhere near twenty million inhabitants. Neither the empire nor the language came anywhere near to coinciding in its boundaries with a single race. East of the Elbe the peasantry, whose status still showed that they were conquered peoples, had once spoken Slavonic languages, of which some islands survived. There were also German settlements of landlords and traders, and in some parts peasants, not only here but also further to the east, beyond the empire, as in the Baltic ports as far as Revel, and in the region of Livonia which was ruled, as we saw, by a German military order. For the history which we have to consider now, the racial distinctions within Germany are of little importance. The same is true of the distinction between the old civilization of western Germany, which went back continuously to the Roman empire, and the more recently imposed Christian civilization of the region to the east. The educated and responsible elements of Germany were sufficiently homogeneous to respond in much the same way to political and ecclesiastical emergencies, whether they belonged to one region or to the other.

Among the states into which the empire was divided, the most powerful was that of the Habsburg family, from which the emperors had been elected since 1438 and from which, in spite of some narrow escapes, they continued to be elected as long as the empire lasted. They had perhaps nearer two million subjects than one. The centre of their power was in the five duchies which ran down from Vienna to the Adriatic. Of these Austria was the chief, and so the Habsburgs are often called the house of Austria. The borderline between German and Slavonic speech ran irregularly through three of the other duchies. Besides these the Habsburgs had wide possessions in western Germany. As German princes they were not so powerful as to be safe from the jealousy of other princes. Like their predecessors as emperors, they had lost much of their constitutional leadership through the concessions which they had made to the electors, the most considerable of these princes, at one election after another. The Emperor Maximilian and his successor had before them a number of projects for constitutional reform; but none of them went through, and the machinery of the imperial government worked very badly. This was the more ominous because in the late fifteenth century the German hold over the frontier lands was becoming less secure. The Teutonic Order had to submit to the overlordship of Poland. The Habsburgs themselves lost their dominance over the lands to the east of the five duchies. They had held together in personal union the elective crowns of Bohemia and Hungary; but this combination broke up, and Hungary became the centre of a new grouping of states. The fortunes of the Habsburg dynasty were not declining. An emperor could still at need become a rallying-point for old loyalties and for the common interest in law and order. The loss of influence in the east was more than compensated for by huge Habsburg acquisitions of territory elsewhere; but these were of such a kind that the Habsburgs ceased to be merely a German dynasty. They acquired territories all over Europe, which sometimes enabled them to bring strength from outside to bear upon German affairs, but more often led them to neglect these affairs in order to pursue their own ends abroad.

By an extraordinary result of their dynastic marriages, the most extraordinary result that the old dynastic system ever produced, and one which affected the main lines of European history until the French Revolution, the Habsburgs became an international power. We have seen that the Archduke Maximilian, before becoming emperor, married the heiress of Charles the Bold of Burgundy, so that their two agglomerations of states were merged. They pooled their strength; they improved their administration together; each furthered the ambitions of the other; but each also had to meet the other's liabilities. The princes who were opponents of the Habsburgs, especially those in western Germany, now looked for support to France, the old enemy of the Burgundians. Maximilian and Mary had an heir. He died too young to make a great name, but he married and in his turn had a son. At the time of her marriage the mother of this son was not an heiress; she had a brother and an elder sister, but they both died and she became the greatest heiress in the world, the heiress to Castile and Aragon with all their possessions overseas. So, without anyone's having planned or intended it, an unexampled personal union of states came to pass. Charles of Habsburg inherited the Burgundian assemblage of provinces from his short-lived father in 1506, Aragon and Castile from his maternal grandparents Ferdinand and Isabella in 1516, and the German territories of the Habsburgs from his other grandfather Maximilian in 1519, in which year he was duly elected emperor.

Many of his contemporaries believed that Charles aimed at converting this chain of monarchies into a domination over the whole western world. Actually he never entertained any such fantastic hope. He never succeeded in setting up common machinery for all his dominions. He scarcely made the attempt, and any one of them would have resented such an encroachment on its freedom. Even if his character had been that of the aggressive conqueror, which it was not, he never would have found himself free to give it rein; but, in trying to maintain all that he had inherited, he found himself in perpetual conflicts on all his frontiers, and any one of his opponents might take up the cause of any other. When religious strife began in Germany he could not stand aside, but that meant that this strife would rouse all the antagonisms of his international position. He was an orthodox Catholic all through his life; but he understood the need for reform. He did not refrain from taking away powers and privileges from the Church. In 1528 he secularized the great ecclesiastical principality of Utrecht, in his Burgundian dominions, and in the following year the Pope had to grant him the right of nominating the bishops there, although their authority was now purely spiritual. But he was essentially conservative and moderate. Government could not be carried on satisfactorily in any of his dominions unless he gave it his personal attention; in every part of them he had war or civil war or heresy on his hands, and as soon as one was quieted another called him away. In Germany, therefore, for a whole generation his ecclesiastical policy was a series of expedients which broke down one after another. In his other dominions, if he enforced religious uniformity he strengthened his government: in Germany, if he repressed heresy the opposition of the princes and others became so dangerous that it weakened him against the Turks or the French. On the other hand, if he conciliated the better elements of this opposition by furthering reforms he opened the way for social disturbances and encroachments on ecclesiastical property by princes or knights. Thus the political state of Germany made ecclesiastical changes cut deeper there than anywhere else.

Reform had begun in Germany before Charles's time, and had even been spreading outwards from Germany, for instance among the houses of the Benedictine order of monks. In German art and in German thought the new spirit which came in from Italy was fused with an indigenous ethical seriousness, so that there the Renaissance quickened the impatience of the reformers. Late in the fifteenth century and early in the sixteenth a German scholar, Reuchlin, won a great victory for the spirit of honest inquiry by reviving Hebrew studies. He began an age which has only lately ended, in which the most valuable studies of the Hebrew Scriptures have been carried on not by Jewish but by Christian scholars. In the course of his work he became involved in a fight against obscurantism. His immediate enemies were those who aimed at blotting out the learning of the Jews; but, in resisting them, he had able allies who opened a general attack on the wilful ignorance of the worst kind of ecclesiastical conservatism. They won their victory with educated opinion by using the printing-press, and so they dressed the arena for the great gladiator of reform, Martin Luther.

Luther was a prophet, a man with a great power of believing and converting. Some parts of the inherited religion were intensely real to him, but there were others of which he was unaware and yet others which he loathed and vilified. His mind had been trained in the medieval distinctions and methods of theological disputation, and he had lightning flashes of penetration into human nature and beyond it; but he never foresaw the consequences of his words and acts and he was forced along from one position to another. He looked for precedents for his opinions among the writings of the previous century, and he found them, as indeed he could have found adumbrations of almost any other opinions, if he had chanced to hold them, but in the complex processes of his mind the intellect never broke away from the emotions. He was no stranger to the Renaissance. He visited Rome and he learned Greek. But when the great Erasmus would write no more against the evils of the Church than could be written, with whatever pungency, within the limits of orthodox belief, Luther showed nothing but contemptuous anger. Yet he was infinitely inconsistent. He was conservative and medieval. He had none of the scientific spirit or the Hellenic directness. He was against the new astronomy, and if his common sense sometimes asserted itself against astrology and palmistry, he was none the less superstitious. He believed in witchcraft, as everyone else did, but his mind ran far more than many men's on fearful tales of ghosts and the devil.

Beginning as an Augustinian friar, he became professor of theology in the university of Wittenberg on the Elbe, newly founded by a highly orthodox elector of Saxony. This elector prohibited the raising of money for papal purposes within his dominions by the sale of indulgences. The particular purpose in question at the time, the sumptuous rebuilding of St. Peter's in Rome, appealed far less to Germans than, say, defence against the Turks. Luther backed up the elector by making a contribution to a long-standing academic debate on the implications of indulgences in general. The discussion spread and ceased to be academic. If indulgences were as unjustifiable as Luther maintained, there was danger for the finances of the Church. If his underlying principles were sound, princes would have much to justify them if they took possession of church property. The Church, as we have said, was a highly centralized body; but it was centralized only for administration and not for defence. Rome could do no more than appoint or send representatives, first to argue, then to negotiate, but not to negotiate with Luther alone, for so many public and political issues were raised that they were discussed in the imperial diet.

Four years after the beginning of his first controversy, Luther had become the leader of a movement in which one of the motive forces was German national feeling. He had been driven step by step to take up the position which has ever since been the Protestant position. Since Luther was almost as difficult to deal with, either in practical affairs or in intellectual argument, as anyone who ever lived, this does not mean that any notable body of people ever exactly accepted any one of his varying formulations of his doctrines; but millions have followed him in fervently believing many things, especially that a man can be justified to God by faith but not by works; that all believers are priests, and so that the laity should receive the communion in both kinds; that priests should be allowed to marry; that private masses should be done away with; that the papacy is Antichrist. These views he spread broadcast in pamphlets written with a mastery of German idiom which had never been equalled; and from his writings and the legends of his sayings his followers formed not only their creed but also their image of their leader—of his joviality, his love of music, his courage, his coarseness, his deep earnestness. He was condemned as a heretic, but he burnt the papal bulls. He was outlawed by the diet, but his elector, though he never became a Lutheran, hid and protected him. In his hiding-place he began to translate the Bible into German, and the prose of this translation set the standard by which German became a single literary language.

It was not only in language that Luther left legacies to all Germany; but his religious revolt at once led to conflict and disruption in social and political life. No sooner was he at the head of a movement than it became the reason or the pretext for disorders. A turbulent knight, who had a private war against one of the prince-bishops, took to theological controversy and gathered about him both armed bandits and venomous pamphleteers. The peasants of south-west Germany rose against their masters, burning and destroying. Luther fulminated against them, calling on the authorities to slay; but his own defiance had done something to liberate theirs. He had shaken some of the beliefs on which the social order rested. For him marriage was no longer a sacrament. That might mean much or it might mean little in practice. Luther himself condoned the bigamy of one Protestant prince. In western Germany there were fanatical extremists who did not stop short of holding their wives as well as their property in common. They seized the episcopal city of Münster and held it as a communist republic for sixteen months, until the stern punishment of the authorities overtook them. Meanwhile one prince after another was declaring himself a convert to the new opinions, seizing church property and demolishing ecclesiastical jurisdiction.

The Germany which shook with this earthquake was part of the European state-system shaped in the wars of Italy, and its crisis was a signal for the renewal of that mêlée. In 1515, the year when Luther was outlawed, a new king of France, the showy Francis I, had a second temptation to go to war in some disorders in Spain. The Pope, again intending to acquire frontier towns, joined him, and so the questions of Milan, Naples, Burgundy, and other places were re-opened. Altogether the Emperor Charles V had four wars with Francis I, and they were followed by a fifth against his successor, Henry II, during the course of which Charles, worn out with his labours, abdicated, leaving his successor Philip II of Spain to conclude that war. When they began the first of these wars, the French miscalculated in relying on the trouble in Spain, for Charles put these disorders down quickly, and the commonalty of Spain gave their rulers very little trouble until the early nineteenth century. The first war was like those that preceded it, but it ought to have served as a warning that the power of Spain was growing firmer at home, and making firmer links with its international system of allies. The Pope changed sides; and he was succeeded by a pope from the Netherlands, a subject of Charles who had been his tutor. The war ended in 1525 with a smashing victory by the Spaniards at Pavia in north Italy, but if the French had not divided their forces they might not have been beaten, and so they were tempted to try again. A new pope took their side. They detached England from its traditional Burgundian alliance. This time, in 1527, Rome was sacked by Spanish, German, and Italian troops under a renegade French general. The Spaniards conquered all Italy; but in a third war the French did better. Charles had had failures in the Mediterranean, which we shall notice in a moment, and the European system was now so torn by dissension that when the French attacked again, it was with the Turks as their allies at sea. But England had reverted to its normal alliance, and the Spanish army was steadily improving. Its discipline was incomparable. Even in these two least successful wars the Spanish *tercios* of arquebusiers and pikemen in equal numbers were the best infantry in the world. The artillery was being modernized. The commanders, drawn like the men from Italy as well as Spain, were the leaders of their profession.

The last war of Charles V was almost a European war. It began in 1552 and it began badly for him, for Germany was by now so divided that the French had a group of Protestant allies there. This enabled the French to occupy the three ecclesiastical principalities of Metz, Toul, and Verdun which commanded the river-routes of the Meuse and the Moselle. The Spaniards invaded the papal states once more, but their general, the duke of Alva, refrained from attacking Rome, and thus obtained not only the submission but the absolution of the Pope. The French also ousted the English from Calais, and for the last time a pope sided with them against the Spaniards. The treaty of Le Cateau-Cambrésis in 1559 made a peace between France and Spain which lasted for a generation, and a settlement of Italy which lasted far longer. There was no new French intervention in Italy until 1597, and although France intervened often enough after that, the Spanish supremacy now established lasted until the duchy of Milan passed to the Austrian branch of the Habsburgs in 1714. The Spaniards now held Naples, Sicily, Milan, and the smaller ports of the Tuscan coast, and they had allies in Genoa and the duke of Savoy, 'the porter of the Alps'.

They gave Italy internal peace, but their predominance was not merely political. Spanish ideas were acclimatized in Rome; Spanish dress and etiquette and ceremonial in the courts of the whole country. The city of Rome saw a new period of greatness in architecture and painting; it grew in size and in splendour. For these wonderful Spaniards were not mere conquerors; they were leaders in the arts and letters until far into the next century. But their power in southern Europe had not been established without sacrificing much of the more widely extended authority which Charles V inherited. It had suffered not only from the French wars and the encroachments of the German princes but, worst of all, from heavy Turkish pressure. In the year after Charles became emperor the Turks had a new sultan, the most successful of them all, Solomon the Magnificent. He it was who turned westwards at last, from the now subjugated Near East, and in that year he took Belgrade. He lived until 1566, and he brought the Ottoman empire to its highest point of power. The two great divisions of western Christendom both played into his hands. Protestants accepted his protection against Catholics, and after 1535 France was his ally against the emperor. He was diverted twice by wars against Persia; but he brought the Turkish danger nearer to the heart of Europe than it had ever been before. At sea he took Rhodes in 1522, and expelled the Knights of St. John, who had held it for two centuries. Then he backed up his North African allies in their sea-war against Spain by sending troops to their support. The viceroys who governed Algiers and Tunis in his name built up a strong power, aspiring to conquer Morocco. Charles V gave Malta to the homeless Knights of St. John as a fief, strategically a point of the first importance. He gave them Tripoli as well; but the chances of Spanish progress in North Africa were at an end. None of the Christian states rendered any help in the western Mediterranean; indeed a success of Charles at Tunis confirmed the French alliance with the Turks. After that Charles met with disaster in an expedition against Algiers. The Algerines threatened Rome and wintered in Toulon. The position in the western Mediterranean, however, was stabilized. The knights in Malta, in a heroic resistance to a long siege, put a stop to Turkish hopes of capturing the island. On the other side the Portuguese attacks on Morocco stimulated the tribesmen there to unite in the Sherifian empire, which withstood all attacks by land from the east. The ports of Tunis and Algiers, with reconquered Tripoli after 1560, harassed the commerce of the Christians by their privateering until the nineteenth century, and occasionally sent squadrons to support the sultan in the Levant; but, in the latter years of Solomon the Magnificent, North Africa dropped out of the main stream of history. The Christian powers could never combine to attack it but it could never muster enough strength to be a danger, or indeed anything worse than a nuisance, to them. Nor did Solomon win any great victory at sea in the eastern Mediterranean. His one important gain there after the fall of Rhodes, the capture of Chios in 1566, was made not from any state but from a Genoese trading company.

On land it was very different. He annexed southern Bessarabia. By capturing Belgrade he completed the conquest of Serbia and then pushed forward in Hungary and Croatia. The king of Hungary, twenty years of age, a brother-in-law of Charles V, went to battle at Mohacs in 1526. He was defeated and killed, with seven bishops who accompanied his army. The Turkish conquests in the Balkans were now safe for three centuries. Until our own time Hungary never stood alone as a separate kingdom but was always in personal union with a neighbour. At first the succession was disputed, the Turks supporting the Magyar prince of Transylvania. He failed, however, to win the Hungarian crown, which went to the late king's brother-in-law Ferdinand of Austria, the emperor's brother, to whom Charles had entrusted the defence of the duchies. In 1529 Solomon carried his war against Ferdinand to the farthest point he ever reached, the walls of Vienna. If Vienna had fallen then, with Germany in a state of revolution behind it, there is no knowing what the fate of Europe would have been; but Vienna stood. Year after year the Turkish armies continued to attack. On his eighth invasion Solomon died, at the age of seventy-six. After his death the position on the Danube too was stabilized, in an illogical position which lasted for more than a century and a half. Hungary was divided into three parts. In the centre was the Turkish province, from the Banat of Temesvar to the Adriatic. East of it was Transylvania, a Magyar state ruled by its own elective princes, tributary to the Porte. In both of these there was religious toleration, and in Transylvania the national customs and the old estates-constitution of the ordinary European type survived. Royal Hungary, where Ferdinand ruled, was a mere frontier-strip, almost a no-man's-land. It remained independent of the Turks because the Habsburgs held it in personal union with their duchies and with the kingdom of Croatia; but this union inevitably did much to assimilate its institutions to those of Austria.

Islam controlled the Mediterranean east of the Sicilian narrows. It had established itself more than half-way from the Aegean to the Baltic. France was its ally. Yet this was its farthest advance, and the affairs of the west, in unexpected ways, were preparing forces which in time were to throw it back. Before Solomon died the Italian question had been settled. Politically Germany was settled too. It has often been said that Charles ought to have put himself at the head of the Lutheran movement and made himself a national leader of Germany; but even if Charles had not been a true Catholic, as he was, that would have availed him nothing. If he had declared himself a Lutheran, even if he had carried with him the conservative elements in the towns and universities and the countryside, his opponents among the princes could have chosen the other party. One diet after another tried to set bounds to the arbitrary reforms of the princes or to meet discontent half-way by inducing the Church itself to reform abuses. Every compromise broke down. The Protestant princes formed a league and Charles defeated it in battle. An unbeaten Protestant elector, who had not been a member of the league, took umbrage at the victorious emperor's proceedings, made war on the emperor, and won. Although their common sense and their respect for the imperial dignity and general interest held them back from some extremities, the princes got what they wanted. The peace of Augsburg, in 1555, gave Germany religious peace. In each of the 300 states the ruler was to decide which should be the one tolerated religion. Thus Protestantism was established in a number of states in all parts of Germany, while the Roman Church maintained itself in the Habsburg lands, in the ecclesiastical principalities, and in some other states, such as Bavaria. The death penalty was no longer inflicted for heresy[1] in Germany; religious dissidents henceforward were only to leave house and home and betake themselves to some territory where their own confession prevailed. So there began the miserable procession of refugees who, in the bad times from then until now, have left behind them the homes where they could no longer worship in accordance with their consciences. For nearly seventy years there was no further religious warfare in Germany. During those seventy years it was the surrounding countries which suffered from persecution, rebellion, conspiracy, and civil war.

All this experience had plainly shown that the dominions of Charles V could not be held together in a single personal union. During his reign he had to hand over German affairs to his brother Ferdinand, and when Charles abdicated, Ferdinand, already king of Hungary, was elected as his successor in the empire. His son Philip succeeded him in Spain. The house of Habsburg was thus divided into two branches. In spite of occasional estrangements they worked together as long as they both lasted, and they followed a policy of intermarriage of which the principle was that if either line were to die out, a successor should be forthcoming from the other. Charles had a choice as to the division of his dominions between these two lines. He might have handed over to Ferdinand not only his German possessions but also the Netherlands. Instead of this he took a decision which enabled the Spanish power to come to the aid of the Austrian Habsburgs by using the Netherlands as a base for waging war against France or for sending reinforcements into Germany: he resigned the Netherlands, along with Spain and the Italian possessions, to his son Philip. With them he passed on to Philip and to

[1] There were some exceptions, especially in cases of Anabaptists.

Spain the dormant Burgundian question, which was to come to life again a few years later.

It was a necessary consequence of the old unity of western civilization that, from its beginning, Lutheranism attracted adherents outside Germany. National churches, more or less on the Lutheran model, were established in Sweden and Denmark. In other countries there were Lutherans, but they were only one sect among others, for the Lutheran crisis had revealed and released a number of divergent types of anti-Roman belief. Among these the most important, if only because it alone became the official religion of sizable states, was Calvinism. John Calvin was almost as different from Luther in disposition and upbringing as it was possible for a highly educated man to be. He was a Frenchman, a classical scholar, trained to the law. He organized the Church in the little city-state of Geneva as a model of what the Church in his view should be; it worked in close conjunction with the civil government of that republic, and it was widely imitated abroad. The great instrument of Calvin's power was his book *Institutio Christianae Religionis* (Instruction in the Christian Religion), which he published in 1539. There was nothing fundamentally new in this book. Protestantism was already formed before Calvin wrote. His work was to define and systematize where there was so much confusion, and to work out a plan for church government and for the Church's place in the world. His method was intellectual; he used argument and invective, writing excellent Latin with a classical simplicity, dropping all the jargon and formalities of the schoolmen. There is nothing occasional or ephemeral in his book, and nothing mean or scurrilous. He relied on the Scriptures, which, he held, are known by faith, and not by argument, to be the word of God. Thus the printing-press made possible a new authoritarianism, and, except in a polemic against the bold heretics who had already challenged the doctrine of the Trinity, Calvin scarcely applied innovating criticism to the Bible. To the history of Christianity he applied it to some purpose. He held that the test of the true Church was not continuity through tradition handed on by persons, but purity of doctrine. In the 'medium saeculum' of Pope Leo I, of Gregory the Great, and St. Bernard, that is from the fifth century to the twelfth, he saw a corrupted faith,[1] and so, from a new point of

[1] *Institutio*, Bk. IV, vii. 22. This passage does not appear to be mentioned by the historians who have investigated the origin of these ideas; but it seems to be a link without which it is impossible to account for their general prevalence among Protestant divines in the subsequent period.

view, he strengthened the tendency to regard the Middle Ages as a period of darkness. His view of the relations between the religion of Jesus Christ and apostolic Christianity and the Christianity of the early Fathers, his account of creeds and dogmas, his judgements on papal claims and Roman practices, were all worked out by acute historical criticism; but in another field his doctrine was anti-historical, for he held that doctrine as contained in the Scriptures was fixed and final, overriding all previous knowledge and all knowledge from other sources. He had no patience with idle curiosity, nor much with scientific curiosity. He did indeed admit that scientific knowledge must be respected, as when he wrote that, although God gave the rainbow to Noah for a sign, there were rainbows before Noah, since the rainbow is only a reflection of the solar rays on the opposite clouds. But such exceptions did not trouble his conviction that he was teaching religious certainties. He condemned what the Lutherans condemned. In intellectual matters he simplified and straightened out what they had put forward tentatively and obscurely. The central belief of his followers was predestination, the idea that each man was predestined to salvation or to eternal punishment. If this belief narrowed their sympathies, it also fortified their will. They submitted to a severe system of discipline. Calvin's programme for church government gave them a fighting organization. The ministers, who were not priests but primarily teachers of the Word, were supported in their assemblies by believing laymen.

The tendency to define, and to fight for the principles once defined, appeared on the Catholic side almost simultaneously with its appearance in Calvinism. In the days of the German negotiations and expedients about Lutheranism, there were ambiguities and uncertainties in some of the Catholic doctrines that Luther impugned. There were openings for concessions from the Catholic side which did not certainly involve a departure from the orthodox tradition. In Austria the cup was offered to the laity with papal approval; perhaps priests might marry; at any rate the papacy might agree to the demands of the German princes and burghers, which the emperor supported, for a council to discuss the whole matter of reform. Reform indeed had, as we have seen, begun in Germany before the revolution, and in the 1520s it began in Italy. There too religious orders were reformed; new orders were founded, and also new charitable institutions. Influential ecclesiastics worked for religious renewal in a spirit of enlightenment if not of compromise. Appropriately enough the spirit of militant and uncompromisingly orthodox reform came from Spain.

Among Calvin's contemporaries at the university of Paris was a disabled Spanish officer, Ignatius Loyola, who had been born a gentleman of one of the Basque provinces adjoining France on the Bay of Biscay. After his wound he had gone through an experience of religious conversion, and now he brought the disciplined zeal of the Spanish army to the aid of the Church in its danger. At the age of thirty-seven or thereabouts he sat among the boys and youths of the Paris lecture-rooms, taking a course in theology. He made the pilgrimage to Jerusalem. He had visions, but they were not of the kind that brings illumination to others. Ignatius did not excel as a writer or a thinker; but he was a great leader of men. In his book of *Spiritual Exercises* he provided a manual not to convince men's intellects but to subdue their whole personalities to obedience and endurance. Eight times he was charged with heresy; but he defeated his accusers. He inspired first one disciple and then another with the will to convert the heathen and to confute the heretic. With his soldier's eye he saw that the way to reorganize the Catholic front was to strengthen the papacy. Before Calvin went to Geneva, Ignatius founded the Society of Jesus. There were years of conflict before the Jesuits, with Ignatius as their general, received their final autocratic constitution under papal auspices; but their historic influence was immediate. In 1545 the general council was at last assembled at the town of Trent in the Tyrol, conveniently between Germany and Italy. The emperor wished it to begin with the reform of the abuses of the Church; but the Pope decided that it should first clear up the uncertainties of doctrine. In the next year, the year of Luther's death, the Jesuits were given the commission of providing the theologians who were to advise the papal representatives in the council. The work of the council was impeded for years by long interruptions and by much resistance from other schools of thought and from governments; but it was already certain that, both in Germany and outside, religious militancy would not be found only on the Protestant side. The Roman Church was not yet centralized for defence; but it had gained efficient mobile forces.

The council, before it finally separated in 1563, did two things. It defined belief in such a way that there was no loophole for misunderstanding or concession in the matters where Lutherans or Calvinists or other innovators had taken up new positions. It regulated the outward and practical affairs of the Church in such a way that the inveterate abuses were gradually overcome. The full programme of reform could not be enforced without the consent and help of the states, and some of them resisted. France never accepted the decrees of the council officially before the Revolution. But, however the states hung back, there were ardent reformers among the bishops and clergy, and before long the Roman Church had a good right to consider itself reformed.

From this time until the present day western Christendom has been divided among churches and sects. The religious settlement that was made in Germany by the peace of Augsburg is commonly summed up in the formula *cuius regio*, *eius religio*—'whose the region is, his also shall be the religion' or 'he who rules the region may dictate its religion'. This formula may be given a far wider application: it describes the state of things all over Europe throughout the sixteenth century and in most parts of it until well on in the eighteenth. There were Protestants, like Henry IV of France and Augustus the Strong of Saxony and Poland, who changed their religion in order to rule over Catholic countries. There were Catholics like James II of England who failed to maintain this authority over Protestant peoples; but these were exceptions that proved the rule. Every strong government, whether Catholic or Protestant, tried to enforce religious uniformity. Where there was no strong government there was religious dissidence; but where there were strong powers at a lower level than that of the territorial state, they determined the religion of those whom they controlled. In many places, from France to Poland and Transylvania, landowners set up a local 'seignorial protestantism', whether of a Lutheran or a Calvinistic tinge.

In a sense there was nothing new in this. Christianity had been spread long before by missionaries who converted emperors or kings with the certainty that their subjects would conform. The Church had been reluctant to countenance forced conversions, and it never admitted any right of the state to interfere between the individual and his God; but, where men were not free, this could have only a doubtful effect. The break-up of ecclesiastical unity in conflict, and the mutual estrangement of consciences, led many men to think of belief as the individual concern of the believer; but even so the new churches, and even the smallest and most eccentric sects, were held together by other ties besides those of creed and practice. Each of them appealed most to some special psychological type of person—Calvinism, for instance, to men with something of Calvin in them;

but few individuals had the chance of gravitating to the body that would best have fitted their idiosyncrasies. After the first missionary phase, membership was mainly inherited. Like the society in which they originated, the confessions were based on the family: they were clans, making a wider or narrower use of adoption. Every religious group has, besides its creed and its church order, boundaries which are related to the boundaries of some other social group. Its place in the world, especially its position below or beside or against the state, must affect those boundaries. Its common life creates common *mores*, manners, and even mannerisms in other matters outside the religious sphere. Its own members will see more clearly than anyone else the religious element in its life; others will see more clearly than they the social and the external. Religious organizations are not less closely intertwined with social groupings than religious with secular motives; and so every religious movement has some economic or social, as well as some intellectual, antecedents and accompaniments, all of which are more easily visible from outside than from within. In recent times it has been shown in much detail that Protestantism developed readily among those who were impatient of the old economic order, like some of the commercial men in town and country, or economically at a disadvantage, like the craftsmen of towns during industrial depressions, and that Catholic conservatism meant the preservation of church lands as well as orthodox beliefs. So it was bound to be; but it remains none the less true that the glories and miseries of religious strife in the sixteenth century drew their intensity from spiritual good and spiritual evil.

Persuasion and compulsion divided Christianity; the divisions, intensified by robbery and bloodshed, were perpetuated by habits and loyalties. There were always conversions from one confession to another. The converts sometimes modified the beliefs of their new associates; but many of them, in their loneliness, were more exclusive in their new beliefs than those whom they joined, and their secession was apt to harden the rigidity of those whom they deserted. There were always men of wide sympathy and imagination who hoped and schemed for the reunion of some greater or smaller number of the divided churches. Most of these irenic endeavours were limited to the unpromising fields of intellectual tenets or constitutional machinery, and throughout the period with which we are concerned they yielded no positive results. There were changes in religious allegiances through the conversions of princes, or the local failures or successes of policy; but in their main lines the divisions which began in the sixteenth century have lasted down to the present time and have been complicated by fresh disagreements.

Nevertheless the unity which they disrupted was never entirely destroyed. The innumerable Protestant churches and sects had much in common in spite of their dissensions and in spite of their different relations to political power, which some of them controlled, while others submitted to it or hid from its vigilance. They thought that many Roman practices, instead of giving access to an invisible world, interposed between it and the believer another world of visible or tangible or audible symbols. None of them had a celibate priesthood or monastic communities, or used Latin as the language of worship. Few of them retained episcopacy or made use of the visual arts or of an elaborate ritual in worship. All these were carried on by the Roman Church, which was thus unique in its outward appearances as in its internal structure. Yet there were great things which even Protestants and Roman Catholics had in common. Even the determination to define doctrine in strict theological terms, though it led to apparently irreconcilable conclusions, was common to all except a few small groups of intellectually anarchistic *illuminés*. It was an expression of intellectual integrity: it implied that, whether he did it for himself or allowed the experts to do it for him, without strict thinking a man's ultimate beliefs were not on the right foundation. The dogmas accepted by absolutely all who called themselves Christians were very few; there were some who kept nothing of the old religion except shreds and tatters; but in the sixteenth century there was still no organized religion, nor any religious literature, except what was or purported to be Christian. There was still religion everywhere: there were still millions whose virtues all depended on their belief in a spiritual order of the universe, in the Kingdom of God; and the secular government, of whatever persuasion, still relied on religion as the guarantee of law and justice.

To minimize the differences between the confessions, or their consequences in every department of life, would be to push out of sight the explanations of much of the later course of history. One illustration may perhaps make this clear. Luther and Calvin, and a number of others who were associated with them, or lived similar lives in other places, were unlike the great historic or legendary persons who had been admired and imitated in the past. These had belonged to many types: the just ruler, the learned doctor, the knight without fear and without reproach, the saint or holy man. Here, however, were men, looked up to by whole peoples and by some men and women almost everywhere, whose claim to greatness had something new in it. Unlike the founders of new movements in the Middle Ages, some of whom had their troubles with authority, they had never been reconciled to the powers that they had challenged. They claimed an authority like that of the Hebrew prophets, and sometimes they recalled the heroes of freedom in antiquity whose inspiration had been merely secular or human. Thus a new type was added to the gallery of the men on whom popular leaders modelled their lives, the type of the reformer. Resistance and private judgement acquired a kind of sanctity. A reforming tradition spread through political, social, and intellectual life, slowly calling into being a less conscious answering conservatism, and at last engendering a belief that revolution in itself, whatever its aims or methods or results, might be a social good.

Within the sphere of religion, however, there remained, precisely because religion is something essentially different from everything else, an identity beneath the conflicts. The deeper we look into the records of religious life, the more clearly it appears. In varying proportions, and with various alloys, the same elements entered into the experience of all the sects and churches. Prayers, hymns, devotional books, the language and substance of worship passed through the frontiers of formulae and regulations, and, unawares, men contended for the same cause under opposing colours.

The richly developed art of the Renaissance was nourished by so many channels from the whole life of the community that it could not live unaltered through the epoch of disturbances. The glorious outburst of creativeness in Italy was at its brightest, and was kindling the arts of other European countries, at the time when the troubles began. Botticelli and Mantegna died during Luther's boyhood. Michelangelo and Titian were his older contemporaries, and they both outlived him. All these painters added wonderful adornments to churches, and each of them had his own individual vision of the splendours of line and colour, of design and of the human form. Michelangelo was a poet and an architect as well as a painter, and he was one of those whom the antique had liberated from the narrowness of the present. There were some, like the Dutchman Jerome Bosch, whose greatness lay in their rendering of the most terrible intimacies of the soul, others, like Giorgione, whose glowing tones and velvet shadows conjured up a delightful world where neither thought nor deity openly appear. Among them all perhaps the most typical, or the most impressive in his versatility and his power of will, was Leonardo da Vinci. The subjects of some of his most admired pictures were religious, of others mythological, of others, the most profound of all, only human; but in all of them he treated pictorial representation as a problem, to be solved by bringing together everything that research could discover about light, perspective, and anatomy. He wrote, in a secret shorthand, hundreds upon hundreds of sheets of notes, with hasty or careful drawings among them, working and questioning as the scientist, shrinking from no observation, however strange, about the nature of substances, or the laws of mechanics, or the nature of living things.

A heavy curtain fell. The wars of Charles V almost put a stop to building and painting in Italy. Poverty, destruction, and danger were not more sobering than the admonitions of the churchmen. There had always been a puritan strain in Christianity; now it asserted itself and men shrank back from headlong enjoyment. Some great artists, the greatest of them being Albrecht Dürer, the German painter and engraver, were converted to the Lutheran beliefs, and brought a new gravity into their creative work. Many of the Calvinists and the sectaries were enemies not only to religious art, with its graven images, but to all visible beauty. The Jesuits had their own austerity. The Italian renaissance, though it can never end, was no more than one theme in the music of the past.

5
The Wider World

ALMOST EVERY YEAR from the early fifteenth century to the middle of the seventeenth brought news of geographical discoveries outside Europe in the south or west or east. From year to year these discoveries were amongst the most momentous of current events, not only for their intrinsic interest and their material results but for less tangible and even greater reasons. They freed European life from two cramping limitations; its seclusion from the wider world, and the scale on which men thought of distances. Lands which had been immensely remote, or even unknown and unguessed at, became accessible, and consequently what had seemed distant now seemed relatively near. We shall have to trace some of the many meanings of this change, and also of another which the discoveries implied. Regarded in detail, they were made by an immense number of travellers by sea and land, whose enterprise and endurance took them, one by one, over the ocean-horizons and over the mountain watersheds, through the fatigues and dangers of one day after another, but, taken as a whole, they amounted to a co-operative enterprise to which not only the personal courage and energy of the explorers were essential, but also the organizing abilities of statesmen and financiers, the technical skill of industrial workers, and the hard thinking of scientists. In comparison with the planned undertakings of our own time it must seem simple, small, and almost casual; but in comparison with what had gone before such a joint enterprise was entirely novel, and it was evidence of something new in the civilization which achieved it. The first signs had been visible long before, but until the movement was far advanced it seemed to be only an excrescence from the life of Europe. From the late sixteenth century expansion overseas was seen to be an integral, indeed a major, part of European history.

We have seen that in the fifteenth century Castile and Portugal were the two Christian kingdoms which not only held their own against Islam but made headway, and we have seen how the Spaniards turned their forces against their European neighbours and were checked in North Africa. Portugal was separated from the rest of Europe by this strong Castile, and it is a curious fact that, although the two kingdoms have never been far apart either in language or in religion, the eastern boundary of Portugal has been less modified by the gaining and losing of frontier-provinces than any other in Europe. After 1479 the Portuguese never yielded to the temptation to nibble at the mountainous barrier which separated them from their neighbours; but they too had the crusading tradition and sought wealth from conquests. They gained a foothold on the Moroccan shore, and they extended it until the Sherifian empire checked them about the same time as the Spaniards were checked. But, unlike the Spaniards, they ventured, from about 1415, into the Atlantic. They took Madeira and the Azores, and then they went southward along the African coast.

Not only the success but the distinctive character of the Portuguese explorations was largely due to Henry the Navigator, a Portuguese prince born of an English mother, who died in 1460 after more than forty years of activity. Voyages were made under his auspices, not under those of the state. He made himself acquainted with everything that books and experts could teach him about the needs of travel, and he used his wealth and position to set up what may be called a geographical research-station. A new type of ships, the light, manœuvrable three-masted caravels, carrying a complement of about sixty men, was designed especially for this work. Voyage followed voyage; it began to seem possible that there might be a sea-route to Asia. Pope Nicholas V granted bulls in which he authorized the Portuguese to make war on the Moors and pagans.

Among the privileges granted by these bulls was that of making slaves of Africans, or, in effect, of taking advantage for the economy of Europe of the slave-trade which already existed in Africa. When the Guinea Coast was reached some hundreds of slaves were brought thence each year to the Portuguese territories. The trade never grew to any importance in Europe, where Africans could be of little use, but it was destined to supply great labour-forces in some of the new environments in which Europeans came to work later on, and to present them with immense moral and economic problems. For the present this was not foreseen, nor indeed were most of the problems of the future, but before the death of Henry the Navigator the Portuguese had already a rich experience of trade and government overseas. In Madeira and the Azores they had established colonies of settlers; they had taught their own religion and ways of life to the inhabitants they found there, and they had set up feudal estates on the European model. In the Cape Verde Islands and San Thomé they had slave-labour colonies under military governors. Within a few years after Prince Henry's death this experience was multiplied many times in extent and variety. The Portuguese rendered to the rest of Europe the immense service of making the first great experiments in colonization, and paid the inevitable penalty of making the first great mistakes.

It was not intentionally that they handed on these benefits to other nations. In the Middle Ages no form of enterprise was safe from interfering rivals unless it could be protected, and the normal way of protecting a trader was to give him a share in a monopoly. The Portuguese derived from the papal bulls a title to exclude others from their trade and settlements, and they did what they could to keep all information about their routes and methods secret. But soon they were so active, and over so wide an area, that secrecy was impossible. Within twenty-five years of Prince Henry's death they were in a much stronger position than during his lifetime. Except for one temporary experiment in leasing it to a company, the business of expansion was now carried on by the state itself, and the kings, having overcome the nobles and prelates, were now absolute monarchs. In Africa new sources of wealth were reached, and a fort was established on the Gold Coast at Elmina, 'the Mine'.

In the same year, 1482, an expedition reached the Congo, and this expedition was in two ways more remarkable than any of those that went before. It brought scientific invention directly into play on the spot. The navigators of ships depended on the stars for knowing their positions, and there had been good instruments for centuries by which they could ascertain latitudes. But the estuary of the Congo is south of the equator, under a different sky. A German geographer, Martin Behaim, was retained to invent a new instrument for use in the southern seas. He sailed with the expedition to test it in practice himself. And the Congo, when it was reached, was the gateway to more surprises. Here, instead of a multitude of petty tribes, there was a paramount chief who ruled over territories as broad and populous as some of the European kingdoms. For the next hundred years the history of this region was strange and wonderful. From 1509 to

1540 it was ruled by an African Christian, with the name Alfonso and the title 'Highness'. His eldest son became a bishop, and there were dukes, marquises, and counts among his subjects. When he exchanged diplomatic missions with Portugal, the Portuguese ships brought priests and soldiers, masons and carpenters to build churches and government offices, and lawyers with six folio volumes of law-books for use in this very inappropriate tropical environment. All the hopes which these things typified foundered ultimately in disastrous military adventures. The Congo became tributary to Portugal, and Angola, farther south, was founded by military force and ruled directly by the right of conquest.

Long before these last events, however, the Portuguese had gone so far that the Congo seemed small and poor. Only four years after it was discovered, Bartholomew Diaz rounded the Cape of Good Hope. Now all the east lay open to the Portuguese, for the seas are one. Chinese junks had already found out the ports of East Africa, and the Arabs had traded along them since the days before Mahomet. The Portuguese knew the way to India from Egypt by the Red Sea and they quickly found pilots who could take them across the Indian Ocean. In the first quarter of the sixteenth century, in a voyage of twenty-one months, one of Magellan's four ships completed the first voyage round the world.

Wherever the Portuguese went they were traders as well as explorers, and, in order to establish trade, they had to protect it by settled power. To trade at a profit it was not enough to land a cargo and buy eastern goods with the proceeds. The Asiatic merchants knew well enough how to take advantage of visitors who could not indefinitely stay away from home. They combined to buy cheap and sell dear. So the Portuguese had to lease warehouses on shore, and store their merchandise to wait for opportunities of selling. These 'factories' were tempting to robbers of every rank and description, and so they had to be protected by forts. Portuguese trade, as it expanded, deposited round the coasts of Africa and Asia the elements of an empire. In 1505 this empire had its first viceroy, and four years later he won a memorable sea-battle against the Arabs and Egyptians in Indian waters. This may be regarded fairly enough as the beginning of the long age in which, until the rise of modern Japan, European fleets were the masters of all the eastern seas.

The second viceroy, the great Albuquerque, was a strong man who paid little regard to restraints of law. He had his failures, but he conquered some of the greatest strategical points of Asia. We must pass over the events by which the empire was completed and, merely noting its full extent, which it reached about 1557, consider briefly what it meant to the world. There was the long chain of posts along western and eastern Africa, then opulent Goa on the Indian coast, the viceroy's capital. All trade with Europe had to pass through Goa, by regular routes which have left behind them the names of Algoa ('to Goa') and Delagoa Bay ('from Goa') in Africa. The most important trades were royal monopolies. On the flank of the routes to Europe the Portuguese held Ormuz, a naval station which protected them from the Turkish power. To the east they held Ceylon, and the trade of the richest tropical area of the world, the Malay Archipelago. They had settlements in Malacca, through whose straits all this trade passed, and in the Moluccas, the greatest source of spices, very profitable commodities which were then almost necessaries to a Europe which lived through the winter on autumn-slaughtered meat. In China they had their own trading-station at Macao. Far away in America they held Brazil; but we have not referred to America yet, and we must defer that for a little longer.

Up to a point the circumstances in which European traders arrived in these new places dictated their policy. If they were to stay at all, they must set up factories, forts, and naval bases; they must be ready to resist local aggression by arms and by seeking allies, they must set up a system of administration to manage these responsibilities. In these tasks, none of which was simple, the Portuguese learnt and inadvertently taught many lessons; but there were others, of even greater moment, in which they had far less guidance from the obvious necessities of the situation. First was the question of religion. It was assumed from the first that one of the objects of expansion was to convert the heathen to Christianity, and, since Christianity was known exclusively, or as good as exclusively, in the context of that European civilization of which it had for so long been an inseparable element, it was supposed that conversion would be equivalent to making these peoples resemble Europeans for all social purposes. In the early days the profession of Christianity and knowledge of the Portuguese language qualified an African to be treated legally and socially as a European. There was no feeling against intermarriage, which seemed to be a means to the effective manning of the ever-widening undertakings overseas. Men of mixed blood commanded ships, were ordained as priests, or rose to affluence as business men.

It was gradually understood that assimilation was not so easy as this. Just as the conversion of the Congo fell far short of the first hopes, the policy of miscegenation created great masses of people in Africa and Asia, and even in Portugal itself, who were not completely European in character and could not build new societies comparable with that of Portugal, but formed a third element uneasily suspended between the inharmonious worlds from which they derived. Within the great problem of assimilation there were many subordinate differences of opinion. Some of the missionaries were content to work within the limits which seemed desirable to the indigenous rulers; others alarmed or offended them by founding schools and instructing women. Some held that missionary work could not succeed without the help of traders; others blamed the evil example of the traders for missionary failures. Missionaries of various orders were amongst the bravest of the travellers, and before the middle of the sixteenth century the Portuguese had taken St. Francis Xavier, one of the companions of St. Ignatius Loyola, to the Japanese island of Hirado, where he died; but not even the missionary work was free from the conflicts of practical aims and the intellectual perplexities which made the reality of empire fall far short of the earliest hopes.

Before the disillusion came, the Portuguese were no longer alone in the wider world. Another kingdom had added to its possessions an empire of the same order of magnitude as theirs. Although on the surface it seems to have been a mere chance that this kingdom was Castile, in fact no other state was so likely to imitate the Portuguese example. They had much in common. The Atlantic ports of Spain were close to those of Portugal, and the two states had both maintained their resistance to Islam. There were other countries, such as England, which had early opportunities but did not follow them up until the Spanish empire was full-grown. The persistence of Spain in the new endeavour is the best evidence that she did not merely blunder into it. Appearances were indeed to the contrary. As the Portuguese moved forward from one finger-post to another, an Italian sea-captain conceived the bolder idea of sailing blind into the Atlantic. Much is uncertain about Columbus. It is uncertain how much he knew about the existence of America. Anyone might know of legends about a lost continent or undiscovered islands. It may or may not have been possible in those days to read of the Norsemen's voyages to North America in the tenth and eleventh centuries. There was certainly enough conjecture about what lay beyond the Atlantic to justify the merchants of Bristol, some years before the voyage of Columbus, in sending an expedition which came back empty-handed to Ireland. Columbus may have thought that he would find the East

Indies; but he may have intended to find a new continent. He asked for Portuguese ships and money, but compared with the certainties on which the Portuguese were already engaged his plans were not convincing. It was Queen Isabella of Castile who became his patron, and it was under her flag that he landed in the Bahamas in 1492.

The first American landfall of Columbus was one of the greatest moments in the history of the human race, but after it one disappointment followed another. Columbus found gold, but no mines. For more than twenty years the Spaniards searched this way and that, but they reached the Pacific across the isthmus and explored more than 7,000 miles of American coast before they brought back any proportionate reward. Then Cortez marched up with a handful of followers from the coast to the high plateau of Mexico and discovered something the like of which none of the European explorers had seen. Hitherto they had found new tribes and even kingdoms, but these had all been primitive, and there was little or nothing in their arts or their ways that the Portuguese or Spaniards could regard with admiration, or even with respect. Now they saw a state with many inhabitants and, in some respects, a high degree of organization. Its king lived in a palace of dazzling magnificence. The cunning workmanship of the wood, stone, metals, fabrics, and feathers astonished them as much as the profusion of gold. This was a civilization of which not the faintest rumour had ever penetrated to Europe; and, although it was so rich in these enviable things, it lacked half of the prerequisites for rising out of barbarism. The Mexicans seemed diabolically cruel and immoral. They were cannibals, and their mightiest monuments were devoted to human sacrifice. They had no domestic animals; they did not know the use of iron or of the wheel; they built on a gigantic scale, and yet they could not build a keystone-arch. They had achieved luxury without emerging from the stone age. Fortunately for the Spaniards the Mexican confederacy was torn at the moment by intestine divisions. The new-comers were welcomed as allies by one party. Cortez was a gallant soldier and a born diplomatist. He made himself first indispensable, then powerful, then master. In three years he conquered the country.

After an interval of no more than two years, high up in the Andean range in South America, another Spanish conqueror, with none of the romantic attractiveness of Cortez, the brutal Pizarro, visited a second, and totally different, new civilization, that of Peru. Here was a highly organized, indeed a planned, economy, with engineering works of irrigation and a systematic regulation of man-power.

Pizarro's way was made easier by the lessons which Cortez had learnt, but this was a slower conquest, and when the Peruvian resistance was overcome it was followed by civil wars within the new Spanish province. But the two conquests of Mexico and Peru fixed the character of the Spanish dominions in America. Portuguese and Spanish explorers have left their traces in geographical names from the cold Tierra del Labrador in the north to the volcanic Tierra del Fuego, the land of fire, in the south; but the empire which the Spaniards left behind them had its centre of gravity in the Isthmus of Panama, with its richest provinces in Mexico, Peru, and the Caribbean islands.

The chief new elements in the colonial problems of the Spaniards came from their having overcome alien civilizations, though they also acquired large areas where the peoples were more primitive. Like the Portuguese they set up a feudal system, and they controlled it by administrative and judicial machinery on their European model, with Roman law, financial accountability, and royal supervision. They had more difficulty than the Portuguese in maintaining control over their officials and their European subjects in general; chiefly because they had so much to do with the settlement and cultivation of large land areas. In their aims and methods, however, the two nations differed no more than might be expected from the differences of the places which they occupied. The Spaniards did not try, any more than the Portuguese, to preserve their racial separateness. Spain had a larger population at home, and so could spare more officials and settlers. On the average there were probably between one and two thousand Spanish emigrants to America every year throughout the sixteenth century. But the Spaniards also needed negro slaves in the islands, and they granted privileges to companies which acquired them from the Portuguese. Generally speaking they regulated American trade on lines similar to those of the Portuguese trade in the east, though the element of royal monopoly was smaller and the corporations of traders played a greater part.

As Spain was the larger country, and the second comer, it was to be expected that there would be a more thorough theoretical discussion in its universities and government offices of the ethical and political and juridical problems of empire. There were divergent opinions. Some maintained that the heathen had no rights against their conquerors; but the highest authorities on the whole accepted the liberal view of the great Victoria, whose conception of justice rested on a recognition of duty to all men. The religious motive among the Spaniards was strong and sincere. It resulted at times in severities to which we should now give the name of persecution, and the Spanish kings set up in America an even more complete royal control over ecclesiastical affairs than they exercised in Spain; but the more central and populous of the Spanish colonies acquired a Christian civilization. There were soon great cities which almost had the appearance of European towns. There were not only cathedrals and monasteries, there was also a printing-press in Mexico from about 1535 and in Lima from 1584. In the second quarter of the nineteenth century an English administrator wrote with truth that until his time Spanish government had done more for the welfare of the indigenous inhabitants of colonial territories than that of any other European nation. The foundations of this imperishable work were laid in the first fifty years of Spanish dominion overseas.

For this we must ascribe much of the credit to the Christianity of those days, and we may doubt whether so good a result would have followed if these conquests had been made under other auspices. Again, the Church did much to mitigate and postpone the friction which colonization created between European states. In one form or another, conflicts of interests were bound to arise as soon as the subjects of different states appeared as rivals in the same waters and harbours. In Europe their trade was parcelled out in national monopolies, and their masters were perpetually embroiled over conflicting territorial claims. If the merchants of Asia and Africa made one European nation bid against another for their wares, there would be no chance of establishing the regulated and monopolistic trade which alone could bring profit from these hazardous and distant voyages. If two flags were run up on one patch of American ground, the territorial rivalries of the old world would extend to the new. When Columbus came back from America the Spaniards and the Portuguese alike were aware of these dangers; but they were able to apply to the same authority which had granted the bulls to Henry the Navigator. In the name of Pope Alexander VI a bull was granted which divided the globe by a great circle into two hemispheres, one for Portuguese and the other for Spanish navigation. This first bull of 1493 came too early in the unfolding of the new geographical knowledge. Fresh voyages soon showed that the line did not accurately separate the areas in which two states had made their respective discoveries. They negotiated a new agreement, and in 1506 the papacy sanctioned the new line on which they had agreed, a line running, to use our modern notation, about 50° west of Greenwich.

Generally speaking this line gave America to the Spaniards, Africa and Asia to the Portuguese; but there were exceptions both in the east and in the west. The Philippine Islands fell to Spain, and Portugal was allowed to develop Brazil. Here the Spaniards offered no opposition, and at first the colony was not much valued, but it was the first colony established in America for the purpose of agriculture. By the middle of the sixteenth century the sugar-cane had been introduced there from Madeira and the export of tobacco had begun or was about to begin. Brazil attracted more immigrants from Portugal than all the other colonies together. It had its bishopric and its governor-general, and it yielded gold.

The resort of Spain and Portugal to papal adjudication on their claims impressively illustrated the international primacy of the Papacy, but even then it was primacy, not supremacy, and there were limits to its extent. Other seafaring men along the Atlantic coasts besides the Spaniards and Portuguese had made discoveries, and other kings were not content to be shut out from all the new opportunities. They did not regard the bulls as binding, and legal doctrines were soon formulated which denied some of the monopolistic Portuguese and Spanish pretensions. There was, for instance, the English doctrine of effective occupation, according to which a claim to territory was invalid unless the discoverer had not merely set foot there but actually taken possession. As it happened, however, neither the Spaniards nor the Portuguese had to reckon with serious European attacks on their colonies before the treaty of Le Cateau-Cambrésis in 1559. Various Frenchmen, Germans, and Englishmen had been active in America and Africa. The English had begun their regular long-distance voyages, and hoped to find a new passage to the Far East by the northern coasts of Russia, but this had brought them no farther than Archangel, far away from the Indies of the east or west, and their still small resources were absorbed by the Russian trade. Something more like a threat had come from France. The French had made notable discoveries in North America; and, during the wars against Charles V, they had attacked his American trade. A body of Huguenots, French Calvinists, had attacked Brazil, but in 1557 their one fort was captured and destroyed. When the European settlement came with the end of the war, the two empires of Portugal and Spain still stood alone and, to all appearances, stood firm.

The most wonderful feature of these two empires, as of the other European empires which have followed them, down to our own day, is that in spite of the immensity of the distances and the bewildering variety of entirely novel conditions their civilization held together. During many of their advances the explorers had a technical superiority which gave them easy victories over those who stood in their way. No one fired a gun at the Portuguese until they had rounded the Cape and worked their way up the east coast as far as Mombasa. The Aztecs of Mexico were not only without firearms, they were without iron, and at first sight the horses of the Spaniards struck terror into them. But in Mexico and everywhere else the numbers of the Europeans were so small that their technical advantages would have been useless without two greater things, discipline among themselves and judgement in dealing with others. Where, as in India and China, the established monarchies were too powerful to be overthrown or even shaken, these qualities enabled the Europeans to set up their factories and to settle orderly relations with the rulers and the merchants. It was not merely that among the adventurers there were a sufficient number of individuals who were suited to take the lead because they happened each to be happily endowed. These qualities were not the private possessions of one man and another; they were not distinguishing idiosyncrasies; they grew from the living European tradition, and they were nourished from the organized life of the European communities. The little clusters of settlers and traders were not lost to Europe. They did not, for the most part and in the long run, adopt the dress, the manners, the morals, or the religion of the populations among whom they made their homes. In time it became clear that their destiny was not to be assimilated but to assimilate. Of course there were deserters, and of course the colonists took over here one custom and there another from their new neighbours; but, even where there was free intermarriage and where the original inhabitants became Christians, it was still to Europe that they looked for their examples.

Materially the colonists depended on their homelands. The long arm of sea-power, which had placed them where they were, could still reach them, to support and to control. They could prosper best if they kept up their intercourse with Europe, sending home the raw materials of the tropics and the manufactured goods of the east in exchange for weapons, or slaves, or tools and machines. But stronger than this material dependence was the hold of their own civilization over their hearts and minds. Among the conquerors there were brutes and cynics, but there were many men who carried their loyalties with them, and so it came about that in these new far-flung communities the kings of Portugal and Spain were acknowledged and, in the long run, obeyed. Methods of government which they had lately developed in the full energy of their rising states were successfully adapted to the new and unprecedented tasks. The administrators paid attention to ideas which were hammered into shape in the universities. Just as the builders introduced the European architectural styles, the colonists in general brought their own way of life and invited their new subjects to adopt it.

In sketching the relations of the European states it will be necessary, from the point which we have now reached, to keep these colonial affairs constantly before us; but before we go on with the course of events, we may look forward and see how the expansion of Europe altered the tenor of life in Europe itself. It had great, immediate, and ever-growing effects in the region of the mind. Civilization was already in transition, gaining new powers and new aspirations, turning aside from some of its accustomed paths, when it was suddenly enlarged by this lifting of enclosing barriers. Thousands of men partook of new and thrilling experiences. Every thinker was confronted by new facts and new mysteries. For geographers and astronomers the new knowledge not only completed the old but transformed it. Physicians discovered new diseases and potent drugs. Theologians examined new religions, and judged the social systems peculiar to the newly discovered races or engendered by contact with them. Lawyers elaborated and codified the principles of property and contract appropriate to the new relationships. These great revisions of science and belief began in Portugal and Spain, and were taken up successively by the other nations of Europe, to continue down to the present time. With them there came a new consciousness of success and power. Conquest on a scale never dreamed of before had brought fabulous wealth and opportunities. For an enchanted hour real life had become romance.

Literature soon gained new themes and new moods, both in prose and poetry; for a similar enrichment the other arts waited longer, but in the sixteenth century Indian silks or choice pieces of Chinese porcelain were already prized by the rich or fortunate. And the economic result of expansion changed the conditions of life not only of the few but, sometimes for better and sometimes for worse, of whole peoples. Even the simplest economic system can never subsist for long together without change, and in the late fifteenth century economic life was as much stirred as political or intellectual life by currents of change, some of them swift and some slow, some deep and some superficial. Among the slower and deeper was an increase of population. We cannot give even approximate dates and figures for particular areas; but, about this time, in Europe generally population, after declining or remaining stationary for more than a century, began to grow. There is little that we can say about the reasons for this change. To say that epidemics were mitigated is not so much to answer the question as to restate it in part. We can, however, connect the change with some important changes in economic life to which it must have stood in the relation both of cause and consequence. We may presume that production was on the whole increasing, since a larger population found the means of subsistence and, in all probability, acquired them for the most part by doing productive work. This accords with what we know from other sources. The clearing of land and bringing it into cultivation can be traced in many places at this time; in others, changes in organization had similar effects. Some of the industrial regions were producing more goods, employing more men, becoming more populous. There seem also to have been more hands available for tasks outside agriculture and industry.

The size of armies seems to have begun to increase: the rise of infantry is a sign of it. Armies were not national. States which had money at their command hired troops from abroad, especially from the poorer countries like Switzerland, where a surplus of sturdy men could not find work on the land. Again, the emigration to far lands indicates that there were, for whatever reason, men available. Taking it all round, and allowing for decline in industry and agriculture in a number of regions, it appears that in Europe generally the population began to recover after its decline. The greatest rise was probably in the industrialized regions of western Europe, and in the lands immediately connected with them as sources of supply for food and raw materials. The increase, at first moderate, probably continued, with some acceleration, until the early seventeenth century, gradually slowing down about the middle of that century, and then continuing only in some favoured places.

The growth of numbers was favourable to the growth of production; the continent grew richer. This implies that its economic organization altered, or rather that certain methods which had been followed only in special branches of business and in special places became more widely diffused. These were methods which are commonly called 'capitalistic', and the period of their diffusion, from somewhere about the twelfth century until somewhere about the late eighteenth, is often called the period of early capitalism. The terms are not the best that could be devised, but they are so familiar that they can hardly be dispensed with. Capitalism means a system in which economic activities are under the direction of the owners of capital or of managers who are employed, actually or nominally, by these owners. Capital has been defined in many ways, but in this connexion it means wealth, whether money or physical objects, in use for the purposes of production. Thus it includes the buildings and wharves, the cranes and tools of a shipyard, the ships under construction and the cash in the pay-chest; but it does not include the owner's private house, or his pleasure-boats, except that we have to include some proportion of their value if his private house is in the yard and is used partly as an office, and if he uses the pleasure-boats occasionally for sending messages about the port or for entertaining business friends. The capitalistic system exists in its simplest form when the owner has the capital completely at his own disposal, when he can shut or open the business, engage labour or pay it off, decide what to make and where to sell it, without consulting anybody else. It does not exist at all where these matters are in the hands of all the workers in the concern, acting co-operatively, or where everyone is under the orders of some authority entirely outside the industry. Almost everywhere in recorded history the ownership of capital has carried with it some degree or semblance of controlling power, and economic life has been organized on innumerable plans in each of which there has been some element of capitalism.

The difference between the historical types of organization which are specially called capitalistic and the other types lies mainly in the degree of freedom which the owner has in his work of direction. A medieval peasant might be rich, and yet he might have no right to sell his land and invest the proceeds in some other piece of land or in industry, no right to choose what market he would sell his crops in, no right to decide what crops to grow, and no right to set up his son in business as a dealer to work in with the farm. There have often been conditions in which it suited peasants or industrial workers well enough to work in such bondage to custom or traditional rules, and a rigid system of this sort has the merit that it prevents both the incompetent man and the unscrupulously greedy man from upsetting the affairs of their neighbours as much as they might if they were free all round. But where there was specialization there had to be freedom. A printer might set up an expensive machine, buy paper and pay wages to compositors, so that he had spent a considerable sum before he had a book to sell. Unless he was rich he must have recourse to a capitalist who was free to advance money when and where he judged it best. In the south of France and in one German district the farmers grew rich by concentrating on growing woad, a plant which gave a famous blue dye. It was bought by dyers all over Europe, and this trade in woad could not have arisen without merchants to carry it to the places where it would sell to advantage, without a trade in foodstuffs that freed the woad-growers from growing their own food, in short without a system of free markets and calculations of prices by various people who were free to sell where the best prices ruled. The rise of capitalism meant the division of labour, the prevalence of calculation, the growth of commerce, and the development of subsidiary institutions which facilitated all these, especially by providing money as and when it was needed.

Other demands besides those of industry furthered the same results. If a king wanted money quickly to hire troops and could only raise it slowly by taxation, a banker, or more probably a banking family, would come to his rescue. The kings dealt in larger sums than anyone else, but noblemen who were contractors for troops, clerics, and even popes who built cathedrals, all helped to build up the network of financial institutions. At first Italy was its home. The Renaissance made its contribution: the first treatise on book-keeping by double entry was written by a friar who was a friend of Leonardo da Vinci. It was printed and versions of it soon appeared in French, Flemish, and English. This shows that the new methods were spreading widely. As the relations of individual men and of communities came to depend more and more on bargaining in the markets and on agreements for money, new needs arose. Above all there was a need for money. Paper money, in the form of bills of exchange, was familiar among business men, and had an international circulation; but for a thousand everyday purposes metallic money was needed, and Europe grew hungry for gold and silver. In the late fifteenth century the richest man in Europe was the south German banker Jacob Fugger of Augsburg, and what made him so was his control over silver-mines in Germany, Bohemia, and Hungary.

These were some of the economic changes of the age of the discoveries, and the discoveries gave a fresh impulse to them all. In those days it was a great undertaking to fit out a ship, to victual it, to provide a cargo and to pay the crew. There were many different ways of spreading the costs and the risks between different owners and merchants; but the far trades needed finance of a new order. The ships were costly; the crews were large; the dangers were so great that it was foolish to send one ship alone, but a voyage might last for years before anything came back to sell, and from two voyages out of three no ship might return. The discoveries therefore helped on capitalism in the maritime countries. They also transformed the map of European commerce. The Mediterranean ceased to be the one highway to the east and became a secondary route, almost a blind alley. When they heard that the Cape had been rounded, the wise Venetians thought of a canal through the Isthmus of Suez, but that would not have saved their commerce. Even in competition with the Cape route, the 'overland' routes by the Red Sea and the Persian Gulf might still have been frequented if economic factors alone had been at work; but the Portuguese did not allow free play to the economic factors. Their naval squadrons based on Ormuz stopped the trade. At a much later date, in the late seventeenth century, the Turks resisted the attempts of the French and others to reopen it, and historians, reading back this obstructiveness into the earlier age, imagined that it was the Turkish conquest which diverted the life-giving stream of traffic from the ports of the Levant. We know now that it was not only to the disadvantage of the Turks but in their despite that this came about. At the very time when they were sweeping forward in eastern Europe, western Europe was growing richer and more efficient and was cutting off one of the springs of their wealth. Egypt and Syria were impoverished, and this may have been the beginning of the decline which, much later, was to afflict the Ottoman power itself.

The Venetians, who had been the chief intermediaries in eastern trade, were now short-circuited. As Venice sank, the south German cities, stages on the Venetian trade-routes, suffered, though they still gained wealth from the mines. Trade now flowed from the ocean seaboard up the great rivers; Lisbon and Antwerp rose. With Antwerp the prosperity of the Netherlands and England was bound up; and their textile industries also gained at the expense of south Germany.

Perhaps the total quantities of spices and textiles imported from the east did not increase notably for some long time; but the American cargoes soon released great economic forces. There were entirely new commodities, like tobacco and potatoes, which were beginning to alter social life in the late sixteenth century. There were large supplies of commodities which had been scarce; it is supposed that by 1600 half the world's supply of sugar was coming from Brazil. Above all there were the commodities which made the most direct impression on the economic structure, the precious metals. First the Portuguese brought gold from the Gold Coast; then the Spaniards found gold and silver in America. In 1545 they discovered the silver-mine at Potosí in Upper Peru (now in Bolivia). There they applied a new method of extracting the metal from its ore, and in a few years they were bringing silver into Europe in quantities that had never been imagined before.

This might in other conditions have affected silversmiths and ladies more than anyone else; but coming at this time it played a part, and perhaps a very great part, in changing the hunger for the precious metals as money into a surfeit of them. All over Europe metallic money became easier to get; in other words there was a great rise in prices, which is called 'the price-revolution'. It came first in Spain, where the silver was landed; then it spread through all the countries west of Russia and the Turkish empire, more rapidly in some and less rapidly in others, as they were able to get their share of American treasure by exchanging goods for silver. Price levels, the purchasing power of money, the relative wealth of different economic groups were upset, and it was a time of economic disturbance. Some men were ruined and others found business difficult, while others became suddenly rich. All those who were entitled to fixed sums, whether as rents or as taxes or dues, could buy less with these sums than before; all those who were free to demand what prices they could exact had new and rising opportunities. So, broadly speaking, the old world of landlords and peasants found it harder to carry on; the traders and bankers found it easier, and capitalism advanced.

All these changes combined, as they persisted more or less in the same directions far into the seventeenth century, to accentuate some of the social contrasts between different parts of Europe, and so they modified the foundations and the power of the states. One great contrast was between a western area where the cultivators of the soil kept a fair degree of personal freedom and an eastern area where their status was steadily depressed into subjection. There was great diversity within the western area. In France and England large estates were growing up, while in parts of the Netherlands and of Switzerland the countryside came more and more under the control of the towns and their merchants. It is, however, roughly true that in the west there was much free ownership and much freedom of contract between landlords and tenants, while in Poland, Germany east of the Elbe, and Denmark, agriculture, especially corn-growing, was an export industry, working for the populous and commercial west, and managed by great landowners, with powers over the peasantry which they often used oppressively.

Until the middle of the sixteenth century the chief political result of economic change was that, in unison with the military and ecclesiastical events which we have noticed, it established Spain as the strongest Christian power.

6

Wars of Religion, 1559–1659

FOR ALMOST exactly a century there followed wars and revolutions in which there was never a genuine and general peace. In the political sphere their greatest result was that Spain lost its ascendancy both in Europe and overseas. Mercifully for the survival of western civilization, the pressure of the Turks was relaxed. The peace of Le Cateau-Cambrésis put an end to the active alliance with France which had almost brought them into the European system, and there were signs that all was not well with their empire. One sultan was deposed and another was murdered; the others, and their viziers, were mediocrities or worse; the court became more and more corrupt; the outlying pashas disregarded the central power. The discipline of the army was impaired, and the janissaries became a hereditary caste with other interests outside their proper military business. Before long the French, by means of their commerce and through acting as protectors of its Christian subjects, began to acquire influence within the empire itself. For the present, however, the main fabric was unshaken. The dynasty maintained itself; Constantinople was unapproachable and safe; no territory worth mentioning was lost in the wars.

There was indeed one very famous encounter, the battle of Lepanto. In 1570 the Turks planned an attack on Cyprus, and, to save it, the Pope and Spain made an alliance with the Venetians. In 1571 the attack began. The principal fortress of the island surrendered and its garrison was treacherously massacred. Then the allied fleet put out from Messina, with contingents from Malta and nine Italian states. At Lepanto they destroyed the Turkish fleet, and won the most unqualified victory of the Christian arms for nearly 600 years. It proved that, once they could combine, the Christian states were a match for the Turks, at least by sea. That was a great thing; but that was all. The victory was not followed up. The alliance fell apart. Cyprus was lost. In 1580 the Spaniards made a truce of long duration with the Turks. The position in the Mediterranean remained for more than a century substantially what it had been before, with the Christians predominant to the west of the Sicilian narrows, and the Turks to the east, where by degrees they tightened their hold.

On land there were frontier wars, but nothing decisive happened in Europe. In the late sixteenth century the fighting was on the whole favourable to the Habsburgs, who took advantage of a diversion in the Turkish rear brought about by the revival of Persia under its great ruler Shah Abbas. In 1606 the Turks made a treaty of peace with the emperor, and for the first time they negotiated the terms instead of dictating them. For more than half a century the emperors had paid tribute to the Turks, and now they bought it off with a lump sum; but they won back no territory, and it was another fifty years before they had enough quiet at home to conduct any serious military operations on their eastern frontier. In 1620–1 the Turks were at war with Poland, but this was a mere episode, and for more than twenty years after that they had no trouble from any of their Christian neighbours. They were left at liberty to extinguish the Persian revival.

In the quarrels which prevented the European states from combining against the Turks, religion and politics were more closely connected than at any other time, both in the internal affairs of the states and in their mutual relations. It was, indeed, impossible to distinguish domestic from international affairs, for the religious parties were bound together by loyalties which transcended national boundaries. They took sides in political and constitutional conflicts, and tried to succour their friends in other countries with the resources of their states. So intense was this militancy that it threatened to undo the consolidation of some of the strongest states. It broke out as soon as the peace of 1559 set Frenchmen and Spaniards free from their absorption in the struggle for Italy. The great survivors from the crises of the early sixteenth century died within a few years of one another, Ignatius Loyola in 1556, Calvin and the Emperor Ferdinand in 1564. The men who were now in office and in power had grown up after the religious schism began; they no longer tried to restore the old unity by compromises, but took their positions on one side or other of the dividing lines for granted. Having inherited the new religious enmities along with the old dynastic and constitutional feuds, they sharpened contention wherever they found it.

The year of the treaty of Le Cateau-Cambrésis saw the foundation of the academy at Geneva, a university on a new model, to which ministers and laymen came from all over Europe to learn the fighting faith of Calvin. When the men who were trained at Geneva returned to their homes they nowhere set up institutions exactly on the Genevan plan; but everywhere they did set up organizations of their own, and throughout Europe Calvinism became a unified political and intellectual force. The final sessions of the Council of Trent marked the same stage on the Catholic side. It was natural that the Catholics, once the first confusion of their losses was over, should win some of them back. In Germany they regained here a building, there a convent; there were legal decisions by which property or privileges were restored. It was often necessary to apply or interpret the peace of Augsburg, for there were still princes, including prince-bishops, who turned Protestant; but the peace was meant to keep things as they were in 1555, and therefore it forbade any further secularizations of ecclesiastical property. In Germany the Catholics lost no more ground, either literally or metaphorically. The conquests of Lutheranism ended with the first generation. The Jesuits, who gained control of the university of Ingolstadt in 1563, began to make themselves useful to the Catholic princes and to make use of them. Soon there was an open Catholic counter-offensive; but it lacked leaders. For many years none of the emperors took a decided line and none of them was willing to use force for the recovery of ecclesiastical rights. The Habsburg possessions were for the time being divided, since two younger branches had been provided with appanages after the death of Ferdinand; this and the feeble character of his successors made the imperial authority less effective than it had been during his lifetime. Thus, although the Catholics organized, converted, restated their claims, the religious peace of Augsburg, which satisfied neither sort of extremists, was stable enough to prevent a renewal of general bloodshed and confusion in Germany for more than sixty years.

During this period of two generations the full force of the great antagonisms was not felt in Germany, or to the eastward. Now and again an emperor or a German prince would take a hand in the ecclesiastical and political strife of a neighbouring country, perhaps as a mediator, perhaps even by sending or leading troops to the help of some belligerent; but not as a principal fully committed to the contest. For Germany it was a long period of neutrality, and incubation. The theatres of war were in the west. In France and the Netherlands the religious strife blazed up and rekindled both old constitutional disputes and the old rivalry of the French and Spanish crowns. During the wars between them each had repressed the heretics in its own dominions. In the Netherlands many of the people, especially the townspeople, had been disgusted by the severity of this persecution, some from mere human kindness, some because they were impressed by the doctrines of the sufferers, or by their patience. The government had not, however, stayed its hand for any reason of policy. In France, on occasion, the persecution had been suspended in order to preserve unity for the purposes of the war. No sooner was the war over than the French Calvinists held their first national synod. As it happened the French monarchy, under a succession of unprincipled and incapable kings, did more to divide the nation than to unite it. Calvinism passed from the seignorial to the political level. The great lords who took it up, some of them in all sincerity, alternated between factious intrigue and a national policy. National policy meant an aristocratic constitutional programme of government in co-operation with the estates.

Across the frontier to the north there were dissatisfied magnates who wanted to increase their own influence in affairs by a similar programme, and some of them wanted to put an end to religious persecution. They looked for foreign allies against their master Philip II of Spain. From Germany they got some little help from time to time; but to Frenchmen, of one religion or the other, in power or aspiring to it, they could offer an inducement that might purchase more powerful aid. The only point where France could hope to damage Spain strategically was in the Netherlands, so threateningly near to Paris that it seemed a French national need to push back the frontier there. There was no chance of setting up a French party in Spain itself; Spain was so united that France could gain no leverage by playing on religious or constitutional opposition. King Philip II indeed substantially reduced the constitutional liberties of Castile and Aragon, and did nothing to conciliate the discontents of Catalonia; but his opponents, or rather victims, had no body of friends abroad. In France, on the other hand, Spain was able, in the name of Catholic militancy, to collect a party and divide the nation. The first leader in this collaboration with the strongest and most Catholic of all states was the duke of Guise, the lucky general who had captured Metz and Calais. He was a person of no small international consequence; the family of which he was the head had connexions ramifying as far as Scotland. These were some of the elements of the situation in which there began a series of civil wars, simultaneous and inextricably involved together, in France and the Netherlands, in all of which, directly or indirectly, Spain took part.

These wars were cruel and destructive. One after another the leaders on both sides were assassinated. In the Netherlands the duke of Alva enforced military rule with a severity that had never been known before in a rich and highly civilized country. The son of Guise touched a new depth of savagery in the massacre of St. Bartholomew. After years of misery the chaos changed into coherent warfare, in which the states kept order at home and waged orderly hostilities against one another: the civil wars became international wars, and in 1598, when France and Spain again made peace, the political, social, and economic map of the region between the Pyrenees and the German frontiers had been redrawn.

In France the constitutional results were decisive. The aristocratic programme of limited monarchy and reliance on the states-general had failed, and so had the alliance of the Guises with the democracies of Paris and other cities. For the future nothing was possible except a strong and centralized monarchy. After 1614 the states-general never met again until the French Revolution began in 1789. The royal officials overcame, one by one, all the local, regional, feudal institutions which had hampered their activities. The only check came from the law-courts, which were manned by a largely hereditary body, with a corporate feeling and not lacking in professional ability.

The religious settlement was a combination of absolute monarchy with toleration protected by special guarantees. France was mainly Catholic, and there could be no future for a régime which did not recognize this fact. The final victor in the civil wars, King Henry IV, began life as a Huguenot, but he was the embodiment of the national spirit which survived the ruin of the two extreme religious parties. He became a Catholic, and sincerely, and he bought off his opponents at whatever price was necessary. Although they had no chance of fulfilling their original hopes of imposing their belief, the Huguenots were still strong enough to ask a high price. In the year when he made peace with Spain, Henry granted them the Edict of Nantes.

By this he gave them freedom of conscience, that is freedom from inquisition, and the right to maintain churches in all places where they had them already. They were to be admitted to all offices and to all schools and colleges. They were to be given political control over many towns, one of which was the strongly fortified trading port of La Rochelle; but they had to give up their provincial assemblies and all alliances or negotiations with foreign powers.

In spite of all the confusion, this was one of the great periods of French literature. In the first half of the sixteenth century the most original French writer was Rabelais, physician and priest, a contemporary of Calvin and Loyola at the university of Paris, who fought some of the battles of the Renaissance with an overwhelming uproariousness, and left behind him stores of vitality which writers have drawn upon ever since. During the worst of the warfare there came the poetry of Ronsard, a Catholic soldier and a companion of the tragic Mary Queen of Scots, a poet of roses and nightingales and of French country scenes. Perhaps no other French writer of the century influenced later writers so much as Ronsard's younger contemporary Montaigne, who used informal and personal essays as the vehicle of sceptical and unsettling thought.

French literature in general became more polished, and this is true of political literature. The civil wars turned on questions of authority and resistance, of constitutional right and the relations of Church and State. The main arguments had been stated in the Middle Ages and restated in the early days of the Protestant Reformation; but some of the French pamphlets and treatises gave them classical expression. Catholics and Calvinists in turn, when they were in opposition, claimed the right to resist on religious grounds and so maintained that government ought to rest on the consent, or at least respect the rights, of the governed. The book which in the end held the field, as Henry IV did in action, was a new statement of the case for authority. It was written by Jean Bodin, a lawyer who, like the king, had once been a Huguenot,[1] but who now formulated the doctrine of sovereignty, the doctrine that there ought to be one supreme will in every state, to which all other wills are subject. France, like Spain, had now become a state to which this doctrine seemed obviously appropriate, and neither of them now fitted the older interpretation of the nature of the state, according to which no

[1] This seems to be proved by N. Weiss in *Bulletin de la Société de l'histoire du protestantisme français*, vol. lxxi (1923).

authority was unlimited, and due subjection to one authority was compatible with some subjection to others.

In the Netherlands the dissatisfaction of the magnates proved to be the prelude to a revolution in which Calvinism and constitutionalism were intertwined with a nationalist element. From time to time the revolutionary party were helped in their civil war by the French and also by the English, who were jealous lest the French might become dangerously strong in that quarter. There was a brief period in which all the Netherlands were united in resistance: a great leader, William the Silent, persuaded them to combine for constitutional government and religious toleration. In the end, however, a dexterous governor regained a foothold from which he renewed the war. The end of it was that the Spaniards retained their hold only on the ten southerly provinces, corresponding very roughly to the modern Belgium, including what had been the richest and most populous parts. Here the Spaniards had to renounce their schemes of modernized and centralized administration. The old prosperity of this region was gone, for many reasons, but most of all because their opponents shut up the port of Antwerp. None the less, although this truncated state, which remained Spanish all through the seventeenth century, was repeatedly a theatre of war, the court of the governors, the palaces of the nobility, and the public and private buildings of the rich burgesses had a characteristic art of their own. It combined the old Flemish warmth and vitality with the proud display of the reformed Catholic Church. Its greatest figure was the painter Rubens.

The other seven provinces, of which the chief was the maritime trading province of Holland, the western centre of shipping and of the Baltic corn-trade, became a new state, a federal republic. This was not the first new unit to be added to the European system, for in the time of Charles the Bold the Swiss cantons had thrown off their old allegiances; but Switzerland was content with safety behind its mountains, and the Dutch republic was the first new state to play an active part in international politics. Although its population can scarcely have numbered more than two and a half millions, its commercial wealth enabled it to build up a navy and to hire substantial numbers of foreign troops. After the struggle for independence had gone on for more than thirty years with the aid of allies, at last none of these was willing to fight on, but the republic was strong enough to stand alone. It began to attack the Spaniards where they were most vulnerable, in their colonies and sea-communications. The Spaniards saw that only a respite could save them from disaster, and in 1609 they agreed to a Twelve Years Truce mediated by the French. They meant to resume hostilities when they were ready, and so they neither recognized the republic as *de jure* independent nor explicitly conceded its right to trade in the East Indies. The truce gave the new state its opportunity. Its East India Company, imitating the Portuguese methods and improving on them, did business all over the east, and especially in the Malay Archipelago. A few years after the truce they had the nucleus of an empire, with a capital, Batavia in Java, and a governor-general. They excluded other European nations from these waters. The trading families, growing in wealth, became a gifted and cultivated governing class, and during the truce the republic immediately established itself as a model of cleanliness and welfare. Classical learning, science, poetry, and architecture flourished there, and above all painting.

The republic shut out the Catholics and some of the Protestant dissenters from full citizenship. They might not hold office. The letter of the law denied them freedom of worship, but they were allowed to buy off the magistrates, so that this was the first populous and developed western state where the sects enjoyed a large measure of toleration, and its example offered Europe an important lesson. These unprivileged religious minorities had little or no share in political power and responsibility, and only imperfect contact with the main streams of education and social life. They had their limitations and their eccentricities; but their freedom to experiment in religious ideas and practices enabled them to awaken receptive minds outside them, and they stimulated creative thought. The municipalities admitted, or sometimes even welcomed, religious refugees from all over Europe: Jews from Spain and Portugal, independents from England, French Huguenots, and, later, Czechs. They helped to stimulate the inquiring, inventive, adaptable spirit of enterprise. In economic affairs both the native and the immigrant dissenters were prominent. While the great monarchies tried to organize their resources in uniformity and system, this federal republic drew its strength from variety and intellectual freedom.

Another European power came into the arena at the same time as the Dutch and partly for the same reasons. Except for brief intervals of friendship with France, England had oscillated between isolation from continental affairs and alliance with the Habsburgs, whose

Netherlands were the great market for English wool and cloth. Twice the English royal family, the Tudors, had come into the Habsburg marriage-combinations. On the second occasion the queen, Mary, was married to Philip II of Spain himself, and he reigned jointly with her for four years. This personal union was ended by Mary's death, and her successor Queen Elizabeth would not renew it. She was indeed, at times in spite of herself, the representative of new and revolutionary elements in England which could not exist in the old intimacy with the Habsburgs. During the price-revolution England grew in wealth and population, and in spite of upheavals of popular unrest the governing class grew stronger. The Tudors worked with it by means of parliamentary legislation and aristocratic local administration; through this co-operation King Henry VIII, and the ministers of his young son Edward VI, carried out great ecclesiastical changes. They confiscated much church property; they assumed even greater authority over church-government than the kings of France and Spain; they closed the monasteries and the chantries. Each stage of these changes was linked by attraction or repulsion with continental Protestantism and war and diplomacy. The reign of Philip and Mary brought a partial reaction, but Elizabeth established a national Church which the papacy could not countenance. The religious settlement was ambiguous, but it was definitive. Continental Protestantism of every colour was kept at arm's length; dissent was punished; but a new nationalism was founded on hostility to Rome.

The same dynasty made great advances towards ending the gravest weakness of England, the Scottish problem. The smaller, poorer, and less settled kingdom of Scotland had naturally been for centuries a potential or actual ally of England's continental enemies and therefore had an old tradition of alliance with France. As it chanced a Scottish king contracted a French marriage during the brief period of the ascendancy of the house of Guise, and so it was that when Queen Elizabeth drew away from friendship with the Habsburgs the Scottish crown was held by Mary, the daughter of a Guise princess, a member of the family which rose and fell with international Catholic militancy under the aegis of Spain. She was faced by rebellious nobles and Calvinistic reformers, and, when she fled from them to England the hopes of the English Catholic peers could not but be centred on her. Conspiracy followed conspiracy, and at last she was executed. This brought open war between England and Spain. The English had been sending aid to the Dutch for fifteen years already, at first informally and then by assuming an open protectorate over the nascent state. They were no more willing to see the French as masters there than the Spaniards. With the Dutch as allies they withstood the first shock of Spanish attack, and the defeat of the Spanish armada in 1588 was one of the proudest feats in English history. For the remaining years of Queen Elizabeth's reign the fortunes of the war, in alliance with the other enemies of Spain all over the world, swayed to and fro, but the glory of that deliverance was never forgotten. It was not followed by a revival of all the arts. In painting and architecture the Reformation had destroyed so much that it took long to repair the damage, but English literature broke into full flower. The instruments had been tuned by courtly and learned poets of the previous generations; now the supreme players took them up. Shakespeare came to London in the year before the Armada. All through the orchestration of his versatility there sounds his pride and joy in the greatness of England.

This greatness lay not only in glory but in common sense. The Elizabethan statesmen kept in sight the need to settle their problems, and in nothing were they more sagacious than in the matter of Scotland. Mary Queen of Scots had Tudor blood, and they handled the thorny Scottish problem so well that when Queen Elizabeth died she was peacefully succeeded by Mary's son, James. For the first time one king ruled from the Shetlands to the Scillies. To be sure, it was only a personal union. James failed to complete it by a union of states, because it was still a union only of heads and not of hearts; but Great Britain, with a population of more than five millions and another million in turbulent Ireland, was now one unit in international affairs. Five years before the Dutch Twelve Years Truce, James made peace with Spain, and his peoples were able to thrive and to quarrel among themselves in full security.

When the French, the English, and the Dutch had successively made their peace, Spain was still the strongest power in Europe. All through the reign of Philip II, who died in 1598, she was so strong that he was believed, with more justice than his father, to be aiming at a 'universal monarchy'. It was only because his many preoccupations in all the continents made it impossible for him to meet them one at a time that each of these three powers had grown in strength. The Dutch made good their first patch of territory in the year after Lepanto; eighteen years later Philip lost his last chance of mastering them by dispatching an army to intervene in the French civil wars.

And in spite of all his losses he had made enormous acquisitions. In 1578 the young king of Portugal was fighting in North Africa against the Moors. At the battle of Alkazar-el-Kebir he was defeated and killed. His successor was his great-uncle, an aged and infirm ecclesiastic, during whose reign of two years half a dozen claimants had their eyes on the succession. One of them was Philip II, and the army, under Alva, which enforced his claim won him two dazzling prizes at a stroke. For the first and only time since the Roman empire, the Iberian peninsula was united, and this personal union, greater in itself than the union of Great Britain, carried with it the union of all the European possessions in Africa, Asia, and America. Spanish civilization rose to its summits. Cervantes, who was wounded at Lepanto, wrote *Don Quixote* to be read in every country of the world. El Greco's genius fused together the solemnity of Byzantium, the pictorial glow of Venice, and the vision of the Spanish mystics. After him came Velasquez, the painters' painter, to commemorate the dignity and courtesy of courtiers and campaigners. There was no decadence in these fields until far on in the seventeenth century; but the future was insecure. Portugal was not assimilated; neither was Catalonia. In social and economic matters there were ominous deficiencies. Spain was rich from the treasure of the Indies, but she had no sufficient industry of her own. She depended on foreign manufactures, shipping, and commerce. While the perpetual drain of warfare overstrained her finances, population began to decline and, especially in the south, lands went out of cultivation for lack of hands. Peace with France, England, and the Netherlands gave an opportunity for reform, and it was well understood that the need was pressing.

It was at best an uneasy peace; the old forces of disunity still heaved below the surface; but the next great outbreak left all these countries outside its range at first, and brought war in the region which had for so long been immune, Germany and some of the lands to the eastward. A good many German princes had been improving their administration by imitating French or Burgundian or Austrian arrangements. Each of the religious parties had become more capable of fighting and more determined to press its claims. At the end of the sixteenth century and in the early seventeenth the two junior Habsburg lines died out, and the inheritance was reunited. The emperor of the moment was out of his mind, and his successor was both elderly and ineffective, but behind the two stood their heir,

Ferdinand, a pupil of the Ingolstadt Jesuits. Another of their pupils, a capable military organizer, succeeded to the duchy of Bavaria, Austria's western neighbour. On the Protestant side down to this time all the leading princes had been Lutherans, and so content with the peace of Augsburg which gave a place in the world to Lutheranism but not to any other Protestant creed. Now the Elector Palatine[1] became a Calvinist, so that a leader was available who, like all Calvinists, brought religion into politics, and who was in a position great enough to raise his German quarrels to the level of international affairs.

At the time of the Dutch Twelve Years Truce and for some years after, it looked as if there would be a European war over a German question, because Protestant and Catholic claimants disputed the inheritance of the Catholic Duke of Jülich and Cleves. His possessions about the lower Rhine were as important strategically as they are in our own day, but Henry IV of France, when he was about to begin hostilities, was assassinated. All the parties accepted a compromise by partition, so that the crisis came in 1618 in another storm-centre.

North-west from Vienna and open on that side, but shut off from Germany and Poland by its mountains, was the kingdom of Bohemia, the country of the Czechs, to which Silesia and Lusatia, across the mountains, also belonged. According to the more or less accepted constitutional law it was an elective kingdom, and, after the battle of Mohacs, Ferdinand I had been elected there, as in Hungary. In Bohemia the religious position was even more confused than in Germany: there were not only Lutherans but also considerable remnants of older national sects, strong in seignorial support, which traced back their origin to the schism of John Hus in the early fifteenth century. Here the Habsburgs tried to preserve the Roman authority by generous concessions; but heresy spread continually and at last the attempts of Ferdinand II to enforce ecclesiastical rights led to a revolution. The leaders of the opposition tried to murder his representatives in Prague, and this was the signal for a rising not only all over Bohemia but in Austria as well.

Ferdinand was almost without an army. The rebels got troops together and appeared before Vienna. They hoped for foreign aid, and

[1] The other electors had territorial titles, 'Elector of Saxony' and so on; the Elector Palatine was so called because his remote predecessors had held a court office (*Palatium* being the Latin for a palace), and his dominions were named from his office, the Upper Palatinate, the Lower Palatinate, &c.

they offered their crown to the Calvinist Elector Palatine, Frederick. He, among various high connexions, counted King James I of England as his father-in-law; but James was not to be drawn into this ill-considered adventure. The only foreign prince who intervened was the Calvinist Gabriel Bethlen, prince of Transylvania, who in the end gained nothing for his allies but added some Hungarian counties to his own dominions. Ferdinand did not take long to recover his position. He made sure of Maximilian of Bavaria and the other Catholic princes, and he bought off the Lutherans by surrendering Lusatia to their leader, the elector of Saxony. Then his general, the Netherlander Tilly, routed Frederick at the White Mountain before Prague.

The Bohemian episode lasted a bare three years. Afterwards, at his leisure, Ferdinand extinguished the political liberties of the country, and stamped out all forms of belief except the Catholic. During the next 200 years Czech culture was put down; German landowners and officials depressed the Czechs to the status of a subject nationality whose language and traditions sank into obscurity. In Germany, however, the Bohemian episode left a legacy of strife. Ferdinand, who had become emperor, caused Frederick's electoral rank to be transferred to the younger branch of his family in the person of Maximilian of Bavaria. This drastic action made many of the princes apprehensive for their 'German liberties'. They feared that the Habsburgs would use their growing power to turn the imperial dignity into a real monarchy. The fugitive Frederick was a symbol, and from time to time one enemy of the Habsburgs or another took up his cause. All this was the more dangerous because in 1621 the Twelve Years Truce ran out, and the Dutch and Spaniards fought again on sea and land.

The fears and ambitions of some of the princes of north-west Germany led them to invite Christian IV of Denmark, a warlike prince who had German possessions, to invade north Germany. The emperor defeated them by the help of a new man, Wallenstein, who used a great fortune, made from the confiscated estates of the Bohemian rebels, to collect a cosmopolitan mercenary army stronger than any that any German prince or emperor had ever commanded. Wallenstein established the emperor's power on the shores of the Baltic, or rather his own power, for political allegiance meant little to him. Even before the Danes had withdrawn from the war, Ferdinand rashly revoked his guarantee of the *status quo* to the Protestants. This, and his new strength on the Baltic, brought a very formidable

antagonist against him. We shall see later how it was that Sweden had recently gained great power round the Baltic coasts. Her king, Gustavus Adolphus, was a great soldier, a reformer of armament and tactics; he was also a Protestant leader, and a statesman, well served by able ministers. Some of the German princes, including the electors of Saxony and Brandenburg, found him an uncomfortable ally. His schemes might well be inimical to their liberties, and they had, after all, a genuine regard for the empire so long as it left them at ease. Gustavus won a succession of lightning victories: then he was killed in battle. The dubious electors drew away from the Swedes; but there were still minor princes who kept the field with them. The emperor detected Wallenstein in treasonable designs and had him murdered; but his army was loyal and it became the standing army of Habsburg Austria, a new great power. The Spanish ally gave effective military help. In 1635 the emperor abandoned his attempt to recover the Catholic losses, and so conciliated most of his German opponents. He had reached an unquestionable primacy in Germany. Only two minor German states were still in arms against him. But it was still thirteen years before Germany was pacified, and they were years of still greater destruction and suffering.

The reason was that the Danish and Swedish episodes had given time for the most persistent of all the enemies of the Habsburgs to collect its strength and to choose its ground to attack. France in the early seventeenth century was gaining energy as quickly as Spain was losing it. Henry IV had begun the erection of an efficient monarchy. His death caused an interruption, but the work was taken up again with relentless determination by a minister, the Cardinal de Richelieu. Richelieu found the French nobility dissatisfied and unmanageable, from the magnates who were almost the equals of kings down to the country landowners whom the price-revolution had ruined. Some of them still stood up for the militant faith of Calvin, and when France fought a short war against Charles I of England, the son of James, it called out the old combination of Huguenot nobles with a foreign enemy. Richelieu ended this. He deprived the Huguenots of their guarantees, leaving them their toleration but without the means to defend it. He tamed the whole nobility, making them into obedient subjects, some of them ornamental and others useful, especially in the army. All this was not achieved without many acts little fitting the character of a churchman; but Richelieu was not entirely out of touch with a strong religious movement which began under Henry IV and continued throughout his own time. It owed much to the

founders of new orders in Italy, much to the Spanish and something to the German mystics; but it bore the stamp of the French mind. St. Francis de Sales, the most cultivated of devotional writers, and St. Vincent de Paul, the most effective of philanthropic organizers, were both essentially French. They had a confident touch like that of the new French literature, the silken verse and the rapier prose, which spread through Europe in those years. The movement in literature was consciously national. The men of letters were gathered under the cardinal's protection in the French Academy: every polite accomplishment advanced the prestige of France.

It was only slowly and gradually that this strength became effective in international relations, but the way was made ready for it by well-informed and rationally conducted diplomacy. First France mediated between Sweden and Poland in the peace-negotiations which set Gustavus Adolphus free for his German enterprise. After his death French subsidies kept the Swedish army in pay. Then Richelieu made a fresh alliance with the Dutch and declared war against Spain. By this time the German princes were so much weakened that Germany became a theatre of international war, as Italy and France had been in their turns in the sixteenth century. The rivalry between the two strongest powers in Europe overshadowed and absorbed the lesser conflicts, and the German questions were only settled when the power of Spain was brought low. Before Richelieu died in 1642 the French had conquered Alsace; Catalonia had rebelled, and the Portuguese had begun a long war to recover their independence at home and in the colonies. In the year after he died a French general won a decisive victory over the once invincible Spanish army. This battle of Rocroi proved to all the world that the ascendancy of Spain was ending. She had failed to take her chance of recuperating after the wars of Philip II. Five years later she withdrew from the German fighting and Germany had peace.

Looking back on all this German fighting since the Bohemian revolution of 1618 historians gave it the name of the Thirty Years War,[1] a by-word in after-times for cruelty and misery. Two things have fixed attention on the recorded horrors of this time. Firstly

[1] This name seems to have become generally current from the publication of Schiller's *Geschichte des dreissigjährigen Kriegs* in 1792; but it appears in the title of the *Kurtze Chronica von dem dreyssigjahrigen Krieg*, published in 1650, of which there is a copy in the Acton collection in the Cambridge University Library. In the following year it occurs in a more prominent place, the dedication, to John George of Saxony, of *Musladini Sadi Rosarium Politicum* (Amsterdam, 1651).

there was the feeling that much of the misery had been inflicted on Germany by foreign invaders, and this feeling grew stronger in the nineteenth century when a united German nation, strong in military power, was able to wage its wars abroad and to keep the German soil inviolate. But it is an anachronism to allot praise or blame to the soldiers and statesmen of the seventeenth century in proportion as they furthered or hindered the rise of a national spirit and national cohesion in Germany. There was indeed, as we have seen, loyalty to the emperor and the empire; but loyalty in those days was as authentic when its object was dynastic or religious as when it was national, and no one thought it morally reprehensible to call in foreign aid for his church or his dynasty. The second reason which has blackened the name of the Thirty Years War is that its total effects are thought to have been injurious to Germany and advantageous to almost all the neighbouring states. Here again it was the abstract Germany of subsequent national sentiment which suffered more than actual groupings of Germans; if this abstract element is omitted, and if exaggerations are pruned away, the Thirty Years War will be seen not as unique but as typical of the wars of the sixteenth and seventeenth centuries.

Considerable German provinces, though remaining constitutionally within the empire, passed to sovereigns whose main territories were outside it. France was confirmed in the possession of Metz, Toul, Verdun, and Alsace. In all these places her lordships fell short of sovereignty, and in Alsace they were so ill-defined that they left obvious openings for future disputes. Sweden took some ports and some strips of territory along the Baltic coasts, and two bishoprics on the estuary of the Weser, though not the great port of Bremen. Thus the kings of Sweden and France now became, like the kings of Denmark and Spain, nominally members of the empire. The Austrian Habsburgs already had possessions outside it in Hungary; the elector of Brandenburg had recently become duke of Prussia, in Poland; the Bavarian house had supplied prince-bishops to Liège since 1581, so that most of the leading states of Germany had interests outside it. In due course this process went still further when the electors of Saxony became kings of Poland, and the electors of Hanover became kings of England. The emperors, having lost so much in the west, naturally paid more attention to their affairs in Hungary and Bohemia, the more so since they had gained so much in that quarter as to become on balance stronger than before. Theirs was the only one among the greater German dynasties which lost any of its lands.

Saxony, Bavaria, Brandenburg all gained. The German liberties were now secure, and if this meant that the empire as such could never become a strong and consolidated state, it also meant that the religious settlement of 1555 was reaffirmed and its benefits were extended to Calvinist princes. The emperors had to reckon with a group of strong neighbours, each with his territorial aspirations; but, although these might lawfully make alliances with foreign powers, they did not aspire to be more than states within the empire. Their rise had simplified the map of Germany and removed some of the impediments to good government.

The political fragmentation of Germany stood in the way of economic unity, but the absorption of some small territories by the greater states made this somewhat less irksome. No noticeable economic loss ensued from the Swedish occupation of the mouths of the Oder and the banks of the Weser. The mouth of a still greater German river, the Rhine, had never been German; but it belonged to men who made their livelihood by trading with Germany. No scientific estimate has ever been made of the economic ravages of the war. Some places were devastated and some were depopulated for a time; but the people were not all slaughtered; some of them merely shifted to safer places. The war may perhaps justly be blamed for the failure of such tardy efforts as German princes made to join in the colonial trade; but Sweden and Denmark also fared badly in that field. It is hard to separate the economic results of the war from the other changes of the time. The shifting of the trade-routes had already drawn trade away from the south German cities; the rise of the Dutch republic and of Sweden had done the same for those of the north; but the shifting of routes, while it depressed some parts of Germany, brought prosperity to others. The great days of Hamburg began.

The sphere in which the war certainly left deep wounds behind it was that of the mind. The Protestant universities lost many of their foreign students and much of their excellence. Literature had no great names to show; and from the early years of the war there were complaints of the infiltration of French literary influences. But even in the sphere of the mind it was more in national feeling than in absolute merit that decline could be noticed. There were gains to set against the losses. The great musical history of Saxony began, and the first German opera was performed when Wallenstein was operating towards the Baltic. Within a generation of the end of the war there were men in the German courts and cities who were famous all over Europe as scholars and thinkers. The name of Magdeburg is remembered for its sack when Tilly took it in 1631; but in 1652 its burgomaster was one of the most distinguished living physicists. At the episcopal court of Mainz Leibniz was soon to display his almost universal genius. In one respect indeed the war cleared the way for developments which, while they were beneficial in some ways and harmful in others, at least fostered the specifically German types of government and character. Except in some minor states the towns declined and the assemblies of estates declined with them. The populace, including the educated townsmen, subsided, so Leibniz complained, into indifference to questions of creed, politics, and morals. But the rulers came to a *modus vivendi* with the nobility. There were no more robber-barons. In the great corn-producing area, for instance, the landlords gave up their political rights and their voice in taxation in virtual exchange for greater rights over the serfs on their farms. The princes were thus able to finance larger and better armies, and to promote a policy of economic welfare by means of an authoritarian bureaucracy. The universities became training-schools for administrators.

Many of the evils which afflicted Germany during the Thirty Years War were as great or greater in other countries. Bohemia and the Spanish Netherlands were perhaps those which suffered altogether the most. Probably the only country in which the universities did not to some extent decline was the Dutch republic, which was not a theatre of war, and whose tolerance attracted students and men of letters from every quarter. In Great Britain there were twenty years of civil war and revolution which, although they kept the country out of European embroilments, were connected with the German war both by diplomacy and by ideologies. The union of England and Scotland sharpened the antagonisms within each country, as such unions sometimes do. In this case the most obstinate antagonisms were religious, and the Puritan opposition in England now had Scottish allies, just as the episcopalian minority in Scotland, which included the king, now had strong English backing. This issue became fused with a constitutional struggle between the Crown and some elements of the English governing classes. King Charles I was defeated, deposed, and executed. The victorious parties formed a united republic of England, Scotland, and Ireland; but it was troubled by sporadic risings of democratic elements hitherto outside the governing classes and not concerned with public affairs. This whirl of ideas and action ended with a restored but constitutional monarchy, holding England and Scotland once more only in personal union, and leaving each to its own separate religious tenor. In the end the crisis cleared the way, as in Germany, for new methods of government well suited to the island peoples; but the arts and letters had been badly injured, and their recovery after the restoration was curiously parallel to the German recovery: science and music flourished especially; in literature and manners there was a strong French influence. This French leaven, indeed, was working in every country from Poland to Sicily.

In after years the Congress of Westphalia came to be reckoned as the first in the series of European diplomatic congresses and conferences in which the peace-settlements and other great international agreements were negotiated. For the first time there was an assemblage of ambassadors and ministers comparable in power and dignity with the ecclesiastical councils, but its members were representatives of states. It showed how far the sovereign states had consolidated their system. One sign was the insignificance of the ecclesiastical diplomacy. Although ecclesiastical principalities were annexed or dismembered by the secular states, the Pope, whose predecessors had claimed supremacy over kings and republics, could only protest. Another sign was the maturity and completeness of the international law embodied in the treaties. During the previous hundred years international lawyers, working on the basis of Roman jurisprudence, had made notable progress. The most famous of them, Hugo Grotius, published his masterpiece, a treatise on the law of war and peace, in 1625. He was a poet, a very learned scholar, a theologian, a historian, a practising lawyer, and a diplomatist. His active career was unhappy: he was a prominent member of a party in his native country, Holland, which tried to press religious tolerance and provincial autonomy further than the more Calvinistic and anti-Spanish military leaders would allow. When his party fell he had to spend many years in exile. He wrote this great book in Paris in Richelieu's day, and afterwards he served the Swedes as an ambassador. Thus, though he wrote it to point out ways of ending what seemed to him the growing inhumanity of wars, he wrote with the hard facts of the times before his eyes. He accepted the sovereign independence of each state as the initial postulate from which international organization must start. He treated the law of war, the reasonable regulation of its conduct, and the rights and wrongs of resorting to it, as part of a wider law which also covers the peaceful relations of states, their contracts with one another and with their subjects, their rights to territory, and all their other activities which can be brought within a legal framework. He died while the Westphalian Congress was sitting, and his book still gives us a programme and an inspiration in the light of which that Congress, in spite of all its shortcomings and failures, is seen to have done something for justice and for peace.

It was, however, only to Germany, Sweden, and the Dutch republic that the Congress gave peace. France and Spain still fought on for eleven bloody years. When Spain, isolated and doomed as a great power, at last gave in to the French demands for frontier provinces in the Netherlands and along the Pyrenees, she gained no respite. The Portuguese still waged their war of independence with French support; and there was no interval of stability for Europe between the end of Spanish ascendancy and the beginning of the exorbitant power of France. Although they were continuous, however, the wars which raged round these two dominations were different in so many ways, and were fought in such different atmospheres, that it is not absurd to regard the humbling of Spain as the end of an age. Fundamentally it had come about because the rest of western Europe had grown in wealth and energy so as to overtake the lead which Spain had gained in the conquering days of colonial discovery and Catholic revival. As the price-revolution and the growth of population continued, her rivals had established their own colonial empires. The French now had Canada and its fur-trade; the English had settled on the eastern shore of North America and in the West Indies; the Dutch were their neighbours in both these regions, and were fighting the Portuguese in Brazil. Spanish trade was harassed and interrupted; indeed the economy of the New World was passing into the control of the smugglers and buccaneers of the new colonizing nations. But about the middle of the seventeenth century all this began to change. The price-revolution slowed down and ended: in most of Europe the general level of prices stood still or began to fall. The flow of emigrants ran more thinly. Instead of expansion there was soon more of organization within the limits which had been reached. And these changes corresponded in some way to great changes in men's minds. Religion and politics were no longer locked together so that every incident in one had its counterpart in the other. A new page of history was being written; but before we turn it, we must again take up the story of eastern and northern Europe.

The Protestant Reformation and its sequel of wars and revolutions altered the relations of east and west. To begin with it gave Sweden a hegemony in the Baltic. Gustavus Vasa, the most businesslike and least romantic of all founding fathers, built a national state round a Lutheran Church, a unified economy, and a monarchy strong enough to keep at arm's length the two powers to which late medieval Sweden had been subordinate, the Danish crown, which had dictated its policy, and the Hanse, which had dominated its trade. The country was poor in everything except iron and copper; but Gustavus enriched the Crown and the nobility from the lands of the Church. He and his successors called in the capital, the shipping, and the organizing ability of the Dutch to develop the mines. Denmark, to which Norway and what is now southern Sweden were subject, also became Lutheran. Its kings had assured revenues from the tolls they raised at the Sound and they made more of a figure in relations with the western states; but before the end of the sixteenth century Sweden had more compact and efficient naval and military forces than any other power on the Baltic. In Russia the Reformation made no impression. Its doctrines were irrelevant to the Orthodox habits of mind, and since the time of Ivan the Great the Russians had walled themselves in inaccessibility. But in the whole region between the Russian mass and the newly solidified Sweden and Denmark, from the Baltic southwards to the Turkish dominions, political institutions, less strongly rooted than in the west, were shaken and disrupted when Protestantism broke in.

Most of this region, sparsely settled by perhaps three million people, belonged to Poland–Lithuania. Here was a dual state, a personal union, in which the hereditary dukes of Lithuania were elective kings of Poland much as the hereditary dukes of Austria were elective emperors. They ruled over, or rather with, some thousands of families of landowners, some of them very poor, among whom the magnates stood out even more prominently than in the west. Protestantism came to Poland in all its forms, including even anti-Trinitarian teachings which no western country tolerated, and by 1563 a diet granted to all the Protestants, and to the Orthodox, rights equal to those of the Catholics: that is to say there was full toleration in the towns and for each lord on his estates. The Knights of the Teutonic Order, whose power on the neighbouring Baltic shore had been curbed in 1466, adopted the new doctrines, in which crusading orders had no place, and so they became a body of German landlords, and they had to conform to the existing types of secular political organization. The grand master of the Order became duke of Prussia, as a vassal of the Polish crown. He happened to be a member of the house of Hohenzollern, to which the electors of Brandenburg belonged, and about a century later his inheritance fell in to that branch of the family, so that in the later stages of the Thirty Years War yet another personal union created the dual state of Brandenburg-Prussia. Until then Prussia was merely a Polish province, and, though it was different historically and socially from the others, its history was of no more than local importance.

About the middle of the century there were great changes in Russia. In 1547 Ivan IV, a bloodthirsty tyrant well called the Terrible, began his reign of thirty-seven years. He was crowned with antique Byzantine imperial ceremony, but he was the first great westernizer of his country. His task was to make conquests by using western skill. He made himself agreeable to the Englishmen who appeared at Archangel and traded up the rivers, but he gave no monopoly to them or to the merchants of any other nation. He bought weapons and munitions from the west; he employed German, Scottish, and other western technicians; he set up a bureaucracy. Thus he gained strength to press outwards in every direction in turn; but his great advances were to the east. He broke the strongest barrier in his way by capturing Kazan, on the Volga, the stronghold of the Golden Horde. Three years later he had worked his way down the Volga to its mouth, and seized Astrakhan on the Caspian. Before he died the Russians held the Caspian coast as far as the River Terek, below the Caucasus. From the middle Volga their traders and settlers had moved eastwards across the Urals. Resisted only by scattered tribesmen who had no firearms, they were pushing across the fertile Siberian plain.

Although it was so unlike the western states, Russia had equal success in keeping control over its pioneers. The river communications through the forests and over the steppe were as difficult and as dangerous as the sea communications with America; but the Russians, like the Spaniards, made one empire. They made good each large advance with fortified lines, and where they sat down at a frontier, as they did before the Turks, they manned it, in that instance by organizing the Cossacks, a kind of feudal cavalry. This is one half of the main theme of European history in that time, for that theme was a double movement to east and to west, in which two great forces, not obstructing each other but back to back, were pushing out, the one by sea and the other by land, along lines of least resistance. But eastward expansion changed the face of Russia's western problems. It increased her need of the west, and it increased her sense of danger from the west. Events on the Baltic coast-line took a turn which threatened to close the trade-routes, so Ivan turned his armies to the north.

Finland had long been subject to the Swedish crown, and there were Swedes there as landlords and townsmen, in positions similar to those of the Germans of the other Baltic provinces. Round the gulfs immediately to the south of it were other settlements of the Teutonic Order like those in Prussia. In this region the Finnish-speaking inhabitants of Estonia, the Letts with their Indo-European language, and the ports of Narva, Revel, and Riga, were governed by Germans, the prince-archbishop of Riga and the grand master of the Order, with, under him, the knights whose descendants were afterwards known as the Baltic barons. The territorial advance of Poland had cut off this region from Germany by land, and Albert of Hohenzollern, before he turned Protestant, had granted independence to the provincial grand master. The Reformation took away the cohesion of this state. When Ivan attacked it, the archbishop and the grand master sought help from Poland, their neighbour and a neighbour whose main trade was with their countries. They offered to submit to Polish suzerainty, as the duke of Prussia had done, but the Poles were unwilling. The Swedes saw their opportunity and established themselves in Revel, which became the corner-stone of a new Baltic empire. The Danes, the Russians, rival Swedish princes, and the Poles all fought one another. In 1563 the Swedes made a short-lived neutrality treaty with the Russians, and addressed themselves to the northern Seven Years War against Denmark, and at times also against Poland and Hanseatic Lübeck. The need for defence against Russia in this war induced the Poles to turn their personal union with Lithuania into an organic union. In 1596 the diet of Lublin made the new constitutional union. Each state kept its own army, administration, and laws; but there was a common senate, a common diet at Warsaw, a common currency, and a common system of land-tenure. The common institutions did not cover up all the strains and stresses between the two countries; but they brought Poland to its greatest territorial extent, and they served the immediate purpose of checking the dangers from without. Unfortunately the union also tempted the Poles into a wasteful and over-ambitious policy of expansion. They took over ill-defined Lithuanian claims to the Ukraine, where they organized the Cossacks of the Dnieper. Until 1648 they dreamed of partitioning Russia and, as a secondary aim, of winning land from the Turks. While the wars were sometimes successful and sometimes disastrous, the constitutional machinery fell into disorder. The monarchy became purely elective, the field being open to almost all comers, and all the nobles having votes. The royal power dwindled. The kings were uniformly successful only in one thing, namely in pressing on the characteristic measures of the Catholic Reformation.

The result of the warfare in the Baltic region (1558–1583) was that Russia remained cut off from the sea. Estonia was Swedish, and Protestant. Livonia proper, although Polish, was also made Protestant by the landowners, and in both the gentry kept their privileges and their German language. Courland was a virtually independent province of Poland. But there was no rest for the Poles or the Swedes. In 1587 the Poles elected as their king a Swedish prince, the son of a Polish princess, and like his mother a Catholic, who succeeded five years later to the Swedish crown. He tried to introduce the Catholic Reformation in Sweden. To keep out the Inquisition the Swedes threw themselves again into the quarrels on the farther shore of the Baltic. They succeeded against their king, whose only success for his religion was in his other kingdom of Poland. Here, at the Synod of Brest-Litovsk in 1595, a new Uniate Church was set up for Lithuania, obedient to Rome but following the Orthodox rites. Most of the bishops and nobles, with some of the clergy, adhered to it, but not the towns or the mass of the peasantry, so that it deepened the social divisions and indirectly weakened the kingdom.

Both the Swedes and the Poles took advantage of the 'Troubled Times' in Russia in the early seventeenth century. The Swedes took Novgorod and from 1610 to 1612 the Poles had a garrison in the Kremlin. Gustavus Adolphus of Sweden succeeded to the throne when they were there. His position as a national hero was established before he landed in Germany, and, although it was not until after his time that Swedish names were famous in European thought and letters, he led a national movement of far more than merely political scope. He made peace with Russia, handing back Novgorod but keeping Carelia and Ingria, thus holding the keys of Finland and Livonia and barring Russia's way to the Baltic. The Poles too kept some of their advanced posts on the road to Moscow for a time; but they were about to lose ground in all directions. They had a war with the Turks and another, much more serious, with Sweden, which deprived them of Livonia and a number of places on the Baltic. Fortunately for them Gustavus Adolphus was called off at this stage to his German enterprise; but they still had troubles on their hands. They began to have wars with the Cossacks. Their prospects of maintaining their positions were poor. The kings had little jurisdiction, little revenue, little executive authority. The army, though sometimes well led, relied mainly on ill-disciplined feudal cavalry. The national policy was one of romantic military adventure rather than calculation. Poland had, as it proved, nothing more to fear from Swedish imperialism; but in Russia these western wars had left behind them enduring hatreds.

In Asia the Russian progress had never halted. Even during the 'Troubled Times' wide territories had been brought under control in the remote northern tundra and in the Siberian plain. When the vigorous little German states composed their differences in the Peace of Westphalia, the Russians had founded one of the great historic empires of mankind. The king of Georgia paid them tribute. They stood on the shore of Lake Baikal. They looked across the Iena and the Aldan rivers at the confines of China. They held the coast of the Sea of Okhotsk, to the north of Japan. And they had abated nothing of their separateness from the west. While they traded actively with the western states, and while they imparted and received a modicum of information, their arts and thought and social structure remained substantially as they had been. The two spheres of European civilization were growing more unlike, and, as the experience of each became more complex, it became harder for the other to understand.

7
Science and Thought

AT THE PRESENT TIME the great majority of those people, all over the world, who think about such matters, believe that among our different kinds of knowledge and ideas about ourselves and the universe we live in, the most reliable are those which we derive from science. There are so many shades and varieties of this belief that it may be understood in a hundred different ways; but most thinking people, and many unthinking people, agree that science is exact, impersonal, and positive, not distorted by bias, not speculative, in short as authentic and as nearly certain as any acquisition of the human mind can be. If they were asked to define what they mean by science they would not agree on every point; but they think of it as following the method and spirit that are most familiar in the 'natural' or 'physical' sciences, that is, as based on observation, on experiment, and on the testing of hypotheses by strict reasoning, very often of a mathematical character. They think of it as progressing from discovery to discovery; as using, so far as it can, all relevant data; as capable of being planned ahead, and as resulting in power to control material objects and living beings, in a conquest of nature.

This state of mind is so familiar that millions of people have grown up in it and take it for granted; but it has not always been so. In the Middle Ages there was not only a great recovery of ancient knowledge that had been lost; there were also new discoveries, fruitful criticisms of principles in natural science, and applications of physics and chemistry to technology, as in the mariner's compass and in explosives. The spirit of scientific inquiry was alive and active; but it was of subordinate importance in the general scheme of thought. Discovery as such was not valued as it is valued now. Many of the scientists mixed up their experiments with mystifications and tried to control nature by magic, invoking occult spiritual powers. Novelty in ideas was distrusted, and the general opinion was that the main outlines of truth laid down in theology and philosophy were permanently fixed, and provided adequate explanations of the nature of existing things. The standard of scrupulously methodical thought was set up by the great theologians, philosophers, and jurists. The astrologer and the alchemist had something of the charlatan in them, or at least a more than normal dose of eccentricity and credulity. From this the orientation of the human mind was altered through the working of many causes over a long stretch of time; but the decisive period was the period with which we are here concerned. Somewhere between the late fifteenth century and the late seventeenth another spirit took possession of many leading minds in western and central Europe, but only there.

We have seen that the Renaissance had an intellectual aspect. The artists investigated optics and anatomy; the closer and deeper study of ancient Greek writers not only equipped Europe with better textbooks of mathematics, physics, medicine, and zoology, but it sharpened method in every kind of research. We have seen that the widening experience of men of action brought masses of new knowledge about the world, and also set new problems which the men of action could not solve for themselves. The new facts would not have been assimilated and the new problems would not have been tackled if there had not already been in existence a magnificent organization of thought and education. It was the traditional work of the universities to keep themselves at the height of the best knowledge of the time. There was constant emulation between them and it was in the universities that the first striking advances of modern science were made. In 1543, in a book which he was permitted to dedicate to the Pope, a Polish astronomer, Copernicus, overthrew the accepted system which regarded the earth as the centre of the universe. In the same year Vesalius, who was born in Brussels and lectured in Italy, published the first modern standard work on anatomy. The new interests did not indeed appeal equally to all the leaders of thought in universities; they never can. There are always some, and there was a greater proportion then than there is now, whose cast of mind is conservative and authoritarian. We have seen that both Luther and Calvin, who had many disciples in universities, looked askance at scientific curiosity, and the Protestant reformation diverted many teachers on both sides into theological controversy; but the original *point d'appui* from which modern science was able to set out to make converts in every other sphere of life was the medieval university. This is true not only on the social and personal side but on the intellectual side as well; the universities not only found the men, they also equipped them with mental tools. Many of the essential ideas of modern science were quietly prepared beforehand by medieval thinkers, including even the idea that the 'absolute' and spiritual are not the only realities, but the material and 'contingent' also are in some sense real.

There were an infinite number of motives which led men to engage in scientific work and to clear the scientific point of view from encumbrances; but we may group together some of the most important under general headings, always remembering that in actual life each of them was compounded with the others. There were economic motives. The Portuguese explorers wanted their new instrument for navigation; the German mine-owners asked questions about metallurgy and about machines for lifting and carrying heavy loads; Italian engineers improved their canals and locks and harbours by applying the principles of hydrostatics; English trading companies employed experts who used new methods of drawing charts. Not far removed from the economic motives were those of the physicians and surgeons, who revolutionized anatomy and physiology, and did much more good than harm with their new medicines and new operations, though some of them now seem absurd. Like the doctors, the soldiers called science to their aid in designing and aiming artillery or in planning fortifications. But there were other motives far removed from the economic sphere. Jewellers learnt much about precious and semi-precious stones, but so did magicians. Musicians learnt the mathematics of harmony; painters and architects studied light and colour, substances and proportions, not only as craftsmen but as artists. For a number of reasons religion impelled men to scientific study. The most definite and old-established was the desire to reach absolute correctness in calculating the dates for the annual fixed and movable festivals of the Church: it was a pope who presided over the astronomical researches by which the calendar was reformed in the sixteenth century. Deeper and stronger was the desire to study the wonders of science, and the order which it unravelled in the universe, as manifestations of the Creator's will. This was closer than any of the other motives to the central impulse which actuated them all, the disinterested desire to know.

Well before the end of the seventeenth century natural science had made such advances in positive achievement, in practical applications, in organization, and in public repute that many able men esteemed it more highly than any other branch of knowledge. There was a definite movement for promoting 'the new philosophy'. Its chief seats were some of the universities: Padua, Leiden, Oxford, and Cambridge housed and fed and applauded some of the greatest experimenters and thinkers; but it also had other means of propagation which sprang from the new conditions of the time. It was helped by improvements of printing, transport, and postal services as Europe grew in prosperity. Its special vehicle of diffusion was not the book but the scientific periodical, which carried the news of the latest experiments and calculations, with tables and diagrams, to a new international public. It also had a new form of organization in the scientific academies, the best of which published their own periodicals. Of these the Royal Society of London, chartered in 1662, may serve as the type. The main body of its most active and useful members were, from the first, men trained in the universities, and a number of them made their careers in universities; but the Royal Society was unlike a university in two ways. It had nothing to do with teaching, and in it the scientists were associated with men of action and men in power. These men, some of whom were themselves more than mere amateurs, kept the scientists in touch with the needs of government, agriculture, transport, and industry, and in return they provided prizes for inventors, a few paid posts for research-workers, honours and rewards for intellectual eminence.

This movement, together with the work of scattered scientists who were more or less independent of it, brought about a great positive advance in practically every branch of science. The greatest triumphs were in astronomy. With the telescope men literally saw new worlds. The work of Copernicus was completed and his hypothesis won general acceptance. A steady advance of mathematics culminated in the comprehensive explanation of the mechanism of the heavens by Sir Isaac Newton, of Cambridge, in the light of his principle of gravitation. This surpassed anything that had ever been done before in any field to bring together a multiplicity of facts as manifestations of a single law. It was, however, only the supreme example of a process which was at work in every branch of physics. Outside that realm there was nothing that appealed so forcibly to the contemporary imagination; but chemistry and its allied sciences were set on sound foundations; in anatomy and physiology a new era began with research into the circulation of the blood and the detection by the microscope of living organisms so small that their existence had been unknown. In botany, zoology, and geology there were no revolutions yet, but there was steady preparatory work, and there were puzzling new questions.

As population, wealth, and enterprise grew, and as the scale of economic organization grew with them, there were many opportunities for applying the new knowledge in practice, and it was associated with many improvements in technology. Technology gained most where it could make use of the new dynamics. Clocks were greatly improved. The introduction of the pendulum into clocks in the late seventeenth century is the first important example of an industrial invention made not by a craftsman, or a person directly concerned with manufacture, but by a scientist whose interest was primarily not practical at all. Pocket-watches which kept tolerably good time were made possible in the same generation and soon became common. Before the end of the seventeenth century the results of a long series of investigations into atmospheric pressure, carried on over a long period of time in various European countries, were brought together in the first steam-engine. For many years steam-engines were few in number; there were none outside England, and they were not used for any purpose except pumping the water out of mines. But in due course steam-power was to become the great instrument of transforming economic life. It was the greatest single product of a general improvement in technology. Not only were quicker, cheaper, and more effective practices devised for agriculture and many industries. So much was done to provide instruction by textbooks and articles in periodicals that the general level of efficiency was slowly raised.

Scientific method was applied in every direction where it yielded results, and the limits of its usefulness, at the stage which it had then reached, were found by trespassing beyond them. In administration better methods of surveying and map-making were useful for many kinds of business connected with property and taxation. They were extended to the delimiting of political frontiers, and in 1718, perhaps for the first time, an engraved map was annexed to a treaty. From surveying it was an easy step to collecting statistics of the resources of a country, and in the late seventeenth century there were high hopes of what might be done by means of 'political arithmetic', as the rudimentary statistical science of the time was called. A beginning was indeed made in the study of population and its relation to birth-rates and death-rates. The idea of a scientific survey of the resources of a country was congenial to the economic ideas of the time, which were largely directed to exploiting such resources to the full. It was used to good purpose, especially in some of the smaller and simpler countries, like the West Indian islands. The Royal Society drew up a questionnaire for travellers, and the method of the questionnaire was typical of the times: it was also used in English poor-law administration, and by inquirers into education and antiquities. There was a new sense of the relevance of systematic and comprehensive information to the organizing of states; but it made no noticeable mark on policy, and the influence of statistics on practice did not extend much further than to make some difference to the theories of commerce and some improvements in insurance and finance. Further progress had to wait until the greater states were able to command much fuller and more accurate information about the numbers of people, their births, marriages, deaths, and occupations, and about imports, exports, and production.

As on the practical, so on the theoretical side, the limits of the usefulness of scientific methods were found by trial and error. Some of Newton's most distinguished contemporaries tried, like the old alchemists, to transmute base metals into gold; and Newton himself at least took the trouble to examine their recipes and consider the problem. It is not very long since scientists wrote of this condescendingly as an example of the fallibility of great minds; but research has changed their notions of the permanence of chemical substances, and one of the pioneers of nuclear physics has written: 'the future . . . holds out prospects of still larger-scale activity, and perhaps the practical achievement of the philosopher's stone'.[1] If scientists have withdrawn their disapproval of Newton's glances in this direction, there were, however, others which they would still regard as aberrations. They are indeed often mentioned in conjunction with the fact that at one time his wonderful powers of mind were darkened by a nervous breakdown. He spent much time in applying himself closely to the study of the fulfilment and nature of biblical prophecies. Since he did not publish his results it may be presumed that they did not satisfy him, but neither he nor some of the ablest of his acquaintances thought the effort ridiculous in itself. With his encouragement they tried to demonstrate propositions in theology by the use, as far as possible, of methods akin to those of mathematics.

We can scarcely help regarding those factors in the thought of the sixteenth and seventeenth centuries as the most significant which have left their traces behind in the modern ascendancy of science, but the scientific movement was one wing of a wider transformation

[1] J. D. Cockcroft in a broadcast printed in *Science Lifts the Veil* (1942).

which coloured every kind of mental activity, and, if it did distinguish natural science from theology and the arts, did not, for all that, regard any subject as less amenable to scientific treatment than any other. This may be illustrated from one small instance which is typical of many. Until the early seventeenth century deaf-mutes were amongst the hardest to help of all mankind.[1] No one knew how to give them access to the possession of speech, let alone to reading and writing. No one could know it until human sympathy for them was reinforced by three kinds of knowledge. There must be knowledge of the nature of language. The grammar of the classical languages was a long established study, but the grammar of modern languages lagged behind, and it is not a pure coincidence that Spain was the first country to have a grammar of its vernacular language and also the first country to have, in 1620, a book on the teaching of deaf-mutes. But in this book the knowledge of the logic of language was joined to scientific knowledge of the organs of speech and to knowledge of the art and science of teaching. More than one of the great scientists of the seventeenth century worked on the problem of teaching the dumb on all its three sides, and we may reckon it as an integral part of their movement that this problem was solved.

When we consider the wider consequences of the intellectual movement, we see that the influence of science in any narrow sense cannot be disentangled from other influences which worked through all the studies of the history, languages, beliefs, and social life of mankind. The classical scholars went forward from the printing of texts to a general study of ancient times, and in this they applied a new and specialized technique of chronology which involved an understanding of the astronomical basis of reckoning time. There were other ways besides this in which historical and social studies became more 'scientific'. Nevertheless the most important fact about the intellectual life of the seventeenth century is a fact about natural science, a main fact so well established, indeed so obvious, that it is often forgotten because it has become too familiar to be noticed. The main fact about this intellectual movement is not that it led to improvements in technology, and so assisted the rise of capitalism and the wealth of nations; or even that it made the first great strategic advances in man's conquest of nature. It is a fact on a different plane from these, on the plane of thought and not on the plane where

[1] There had been remarkable attempts and anticipations, and finger-language was used in the Middle Ages, but what follows in this paragraph is substantially true.

that he could not forgive Descartes, because after bringing in God to set the world in motion by a twist of His finger and thumb, he had no further use for Him in his philosophy.

Although no one succeeded in fusing scientific with theological opinions, it was impossible to keep them altogether apart. The belief in miracles was shaken. During the controversies of the Reformation many Protestant writers had criticized the miracles of the Church, that is all the miracles from the end of the Apostolic age. Although they still accepted the miracles of the Bible as facts, and as evidence of revelation, they had turned two kinds of criticism against later miracles which might be applied elsewhere. They had disputed the evidence for some of them as facts, and they had doubted the others on grounds of inherent improbability. Bit by bit a long chain of writers proved that all the phenomena of witchcraft could be accounted for without belief in the evil powers which it professed to invoke. There was no lack of theologians and lawyers to argue on the other side, and there were outbreaks of witch-hunting in the seventeenth century in France and the Protestant countries of Europe other than Holland, and in America; but the first quarter of the eighteenth saw the practice virtually ended so far as lay and ecclesiastical courts of law were concerned, and the last recorded judicial execution for sorcery came in 1782, in Switzerland. In the meantime science directed a third battering-ram against some of the supposed irruptions of the miraculous into daily life. This was the belief in laws of nature which were incompatible with the supernatural origin of certain events. During the sixteenth century astrology, a relic of what had once been the best available theory for explaining the course of human life, suffered damaging criticism from common sense. Calvin was against it as well as some of the humanists. In the seventeenth it was deprived of the last vestiges of its astronomical groundwork and sank to the status of a superstition. Even then there still remained signs and wonders in the heavens, and wise men still justifiably expected pestilence or public calamities when a comet appeared. That was ended when Halley calculated the orbit of the comet of 1682, which now bears his name, and so proved that these appearances could be predicted, and were as natural as eclipses, which had once been equally terrible.

Thus the frontiers of the miraculous and the mysterious seemed to be driven back, but even at the end of the seventeenth century it was not safe to express unrestricted scepticism. In Holland, most liberal of the western countries, the philosopher Spinoza published a book in 1670, interpreting the Old Testament entirely in terms of natural laws; but there were threatening protests, and no one in that generation ventured to write about the New Testament in that way. In 1698 the English parliament, of which Sir Isaac Newton had been and was again to be a member, passed an Act which made it a penal offence to deny the divinity of Christ. After Newton's death it was found from his unpublished papers that he himself did not believe in the doctrine of the Trinity as he understood it; but this fact was not clearly published until the twentieth century.

We know that many men were more unorthodox in private than they dared or cared to be in public. This was one of the reasons for the emergence of religious toleration. There were others, varying with times and places. We have seen how different kinds and degrees of toleration appeared in France, the Dutch republic, the eastern European countries, and England. Freedom of conscience was the most generally admitted; freedom of worship seldom; freedom of speech exceptionally and incompletely. The Dutch and the English were the only nations among whom they were firmly rooted. But, except in the countries where one stern creed was dominant, like Catholic Spain and Lutheran Sweden, they made some headway everywhere. The sects cried out for them and the churches acquiesced when they were granted by the states. Some men were disgusted by the uncharitableness of theological disputants; others, including men of strong religious feeling, were indifferent to the points at issue. It was in the seventeenth century that the phrase was coined: 'In essentials unity, in non-essentials liberty, in all things charity.'

Since toleration and open-mindedness were growing, the way was open at last for new influences from the world outside to work on western civilization, and they came in full flood when the wider world came to be known and at the same time ceased to be feared. There was now no part of the world from which the west was not able and eager to learn. The wealth and antiquity of the great eastern monarchies, and the marvels of oriental art, seemed to surpass anything in Europe. One of Newton's most admired contemporaries wrote of 'the most civilized nations of the world (such as anciently the Greeks and Romans and now the Chineses and East Indians)'. During his lifetime eastern designs were imitated in European textiles and china and silver; Rembrandt copied Moghul drawings; delicate new crafts were introduced from Japan. But these influences on the arts were superficial and trivial in comparison with the influences on literature and thought. The whole of the east was not merely observed but studied. Among the languages Arabic was studied most thoroughly, partly because, as a Semitic language, it was akin to Hebrew, which was already taught in universities; partly because Arabic learning in general was related to biblical studies. Altogether many Asiatic languages were learnt, as were those of Africa and America, first for the purposes of Christian missions, and in the second place for those of business and administration. Not only were they learnt: type was cast for a number of them, and books were printed. These were momentous innovations in the countries where Christian missionaries worked, and they stand for something of the greatest importance for the history of the world. Even when they investigated ancient civilizations like those of Asia, which were rich in records and in a learned literature of their own, the western scholars were able to learn many things about them which no one had been able to learn before. They brought to bear not only the printing-press but the whole of their developed skill in research, their knowledge of language, of chronology, of natural science, of everything which could interpret the new material. They were able to compare the civilizations of the east as no oriental had ever compared them, and they were able to do it the better for their own newly won objectivity and openness of mind.

The rise of oriental studies made its first great impressions on the European mind in the spheres of theology and what we now call comparative religion. In the same year in which Copernicus and Vesalius published their books there appeared the first printed Latin translation of the Koran. Before the end of the seventeenth century at least one of the Islamic mystical and philosophical books was very widely known in translations in the west. So were the Analects of Confucius. It had always been conceded by Catholic theologians, and by at least some Protestants, that religion did not consist solely in what was revealed, but that there was natural religion and natural theology. On its theological side the tendency towards toleration was closely related to a tendency to lay stress on the beliefs which the various kinds of Christians had in common rather than on those in which they differed. The discovery of unsuspected wisdom and spiritual depth in the alien religions gave this tendency a wider extension, and this came about at a time when the unaided human mind was asserting for itself a higher place than ever before in the discovery of truth. Thus many men came to hold that the surest and most valuable truths were those which formed the highest common factor of the religions of the great civilizations. In other words they were guaranteed by the faculty which worked equally in all of these and in secular science and learning as well, the faculty which was known as reason.

Different people understood 'reason' and 'reasonableness' in many different senses; but to a greater or less degree they were contrasted not only with passion and absurdity, but also with mystery and revelation. A reasonable faith was apt to mean a consistent and beneficent but moderate, intelligible, and unemphatic creed accommodating itself easily to the fashionable, intellectual and practical requirements of the age. As the seventeenth century melted into the eighteenth all the underground opinions came out into the open. Unitarianism gained ground, and alongside of it deism, which retained the god of the scientists as an object of worship, but no longer accorded any primacy or uniqueness to Christianity among the religions. There were also many who openly professed themselves atheists, and many sermons were preached against them; but irreligion was still generally identified with immorality, and atheism was rather a negation by individual rebels than a combined movement against religion itself. In the first quarter of the eighteenth century it was still generally assumed by the governing classes that religion was the cement of society, and there was no interference with the religious ceremonies and oaths by which that assumption was made effective. In one respect, however, the scepticism and criticism of this period brought about a new kind of division in western civilization: Christian beliefs and institutions as such were challenged in the name of religion.

Besides the isolated rebels and blasphemers who defied authority at every point and for every sort of reason, there had always been heretics who claimed to stand for a purer Christianity than that which they saw about them. There had also been quasi-religions, fantastic or distorted anti-Christian practices. Now, however, there were many serious and high-minded men among the educated classes who rejected the dogmas of Christianity and found a religious value in beliefs drawn from various other sources which they tended to work together into a coherent body. A number of streams of thought were converging. Some of them ran off into backwaters, some were dammed back and sent down only a trickle, some were swift and others slow; they were different in colour after they joined; they swept along wreckage with them which made it hard to distinguish one from another; the main channel was tortuous and overflowed its banks, but its direction was unmistakable. Like all new movements of thought it carried over much from the old. It carried on from Christianity the humanitarianism, the will to diminish suffering, which had been growing more articulate in charitable and educational enterprises. Some of the beliefs which it reaffirmed had been carried down from pre-Christian thought by Christian thinkers, such as the belief of the Stoics that the human race was one and that all men had their rights. But in other ways it turned away from Christianity. It repudiated the doctrine of original sin, and preferred an optimistic view of human nature. Such a view can be traced far back; Erasmus sometimes leaned towards it; but now, in spite of the evidence, primitive man was idealized, and a glow of sentiment lit the ages 'when wild in woods the noble savage ran'.

Strangely enough this illusion joined hands with the other illusory confidence in human nature which was engendered by the successes of natural science. The literary men of most of the western countries carried on a long controversy on the respective merits of the ancients and the moderns. There was no denying that the moderns had surpassed the ancient Greeks and Romans in knowledge, and the general opinion gained ground that they were superior all round. Thus the belief in progress arose. The general course of history, considered more broadly than in the days when the Middle Ages had appeared to be a thousand years of retrogression, seemed on the whole to be a process of improvement. This process seemed to express the nature of a divine principle working in it, and it seemed the highest duty to help it forward. The most famous of the Dutch scientists took as his motto: 'The world is my country; to promote science my religion'.

If it was a religion, it was no substitute for the historic religions. It was not concerned with the same needs of individual men and women. It had no church, no organization, and no buildings, for it had not captured the scientific academies and made them its conventicles. It had no liturgy, no ritual, no art or ornaments, and no hierarchy. It was not a society. It had not yet extended beyond the circles of highly educated men, and for the most part it was expressed in their peculiar language. Its adepts made no attempt to convert the masses or to sponsor their discontents, still less to rouse them against their masters, among whom were these adepts themselves. At the same time it was at many points in opposition, if not to the existing order, still to the ruling beliefs. It provided grounds for criticizing mystical visions and ascetic practices, ecclesiastical repression, whether by the Catholic inquisition or by the Calvinist consistories, and the whole fabric of authority in matters of belief. It professed to appeal against the imperfections of Christianity, or the deceits of churchmen, to a higher truth, and when its votaries suffered, as many of them did, from social disapproval or official censure, or even worse, they were fortified by moral indignation. The time was not long distant when they would find allies and followers among other opponents of things as they were.

For the present this tendency was aristocratic, and so was the whole intellectual movement from which it arose. It made its contribution to polite literature. Some excellent writers, especially in France, wrote treatises on science for gentlemen and ladies, and there were some schools, though they were exceptional, where boys were taught some of the new subjects; but in education the movement had only a limited effect. In the maritime countries schools of navigation were founded; but, except in these, technological instruction was still imparted by means of apprenticeship, and the new methods percolated downwards through the employers of labour. It was a consequence less of the advance of science than of the growing scale and complexity of commerce and industry that far more people in the busier countries, down to skilled craftsmen, learnt elementary mathematics. Shopkeepers did their sums on paper; the abacus and the casting-board were relegated to the nursery. Gunners ceased to call their pieces by picturesque names like 'cannons petro' and 'bastard cannons', and began to talk about 'twenty-four-pounders' and 'forty-two-pounders'. Until this time the only way of distinguishing the houses in a street was by carved or painted signs, such as we still have for inns and barbers' shops. It is said that as early as 1512 someone in Paris tried to do it by numbering the houses, but the attempt was a failure. In 1708 a London topographer wrote that 'in Prescott Street, Goodman's Fields, instead of signs the houses are distinguished by numbers, as the staircases in the Inns of Court and Chancery'. But popular education did not go far enough for the numbering of houses to become a general practice in any European city until the late eighteenth century.

In various countries, it is true, schools were opened for the children of artisans and labourers, and this development coincided roughly in time with the great intellectual movement, but there seems to be no reason for supposing that the two were closely connected. The contemporaneous increase of economic needs and opportunities explains some of the foundations of schools, and most of the others would not have been founded if it had not been for religious reasons. In the countries where Calvinism was strong, for instance in Scotland, attempts were made to provide every parish with its school, in order that every man and woman might learn to read the Bible. The same motive operated, no doubt with an admixture of others, in other environments besides that of Calvinism and Bible-reading. In France a newly founded religious order opened many schools for the poor. In due time these institutions were to be linked up with others which sprang from the intellectual movement; but for the time being its influence was circumscribed, and so far from doing anything to efface the differences of educational level which separated the more fortunate from the underprivileged, it accentuated them and gave the privileged a still greater advantage.

8
The Wealth of Nations and the Power of States

THROUGHOUT THE SIXTEENTH and seventeenth centuries, and on into the eighteenth, there continued the long-drawn processes of early capitalism, each sometimes helping the others forward but sometimes delaying them or masking them from view. Population grew. One rough estimate, as good as another in this poorly lighted field, is that Europe, the whole continent west of the Ural Mountains, had about 95 million inhabitants in 1600 and about 130 millions in 1700, whereas in 1930 it had about 475 millions.

There was at the same time a steady, though not spectacular, improvement in transport. In all the more prosperous countries roads, with their appurtenances such as coaches, stage-wagons, and inns, were improved, as were the breeds of horses for riding, for hauling vehicles, and for carrying packs. There were ships with better rigging and better lines; there were more ships and larger ships. Harbours and docks were made more commodious. Rivers were cleared for navigation, and some of them were connected by canals. Every improvement in transport enabled a greater number of sellers to bring their wares to the same markets, and so it enabled those who could produce more cheaply and in larger quantities to undersell their competitors. It tended to concentrate the production of each commodity in those places which were best suited for it, whether by their situation or by their ready access to materials or by the cheapness or the exceptional skill of their labour. Thus it drew together large numbers of people employed in the same occupations or in occupations which dovetailed in with one another, draining them away from regions which could not produce for distant markets: it differentiated the regions. The manufacturing districts and the districts which exported agricultural produce became more specialized, and much of the increase of population was concentrated in them, while other places lost in numbers, and many people were unaware that the total population was rising.

Some great industries needed to be near wood and water, and so in many parts of Europe the industrial districts consisted not of towns but of scattered villages or settlements in the countryside. In the textile industries water-mills were used for fulling and other finishing processes; they were coming to be used for the elaborate and newly invented Italian machinery for 'throwing' silk. The metal industries used great quantities of wood for fuel and so they flourished where the mines were near the forests: it was only in a few places, especially in England, that coal was used as fuel in industry. Commerce, however, unlike industry, built up the towns everywhere: its nature is to bring goods together at points where they can be sorted, graded, and marketed, and from which they can be dispersed to the best advantage. Town life seems to have become healthier as the towns grew in size. This is hard to account for, because medical knowledge was growing only slowly, and there was nothing like the great movement of sanitation which arose in later times; but from about the middle of the seventeenth century there were more and better doctors and hospitals, and practically all of them were in the towns. Perhaps the cause was better diet. There seems to be evidence from English, French, German, and Swiss towns that death-rates fell between 1550 and 1720. They were still very high, especially the rate of infant mortality, and every country was still liable to periodical famines and fierce epidemics; but the new interest in the statistics of population arose, perhaps not accidentally, when human skill and foresight were beginning to influence the numbers of the people and the length of their lives.

Politicians thought much about these figures, and aspired to control them, indeed their ambition to do this outran what was possible in those days of loose organization. It was the general opinion that a dense population was conducive to wealth. There were phases of economic depression in which the contrary opinion was heard, as when enthusiasts for colonization advocated emigration as a means of relieving unemployment and overpopulation; but in the second half of the seventeenth century Europe needed men; the stream of emigrants to America ran much less strongly, and the general desire for dense population was justifiable. Politicians had another reason for favouring it besides the purely economic reason. A large population was the basis of military strength. As the continent grew richer and more populous, the scale of warfare increased. Armies became larger. It seems that for more than a century after the last years of Charles V no general commanded more than 50,000 men in the field; but during the great wars which began in the 1660s there was a rise in numbers, so that the French and the coalition opposed to them each had armies far exceeding 100,000. These were not national armies. They still consisted of mercenary troops recruited from every country where pay acted as an inducement to serve; but the national element was coming in. The stronger states, with their new mastery of administrative method, prevented their subjects from serving under any flag except their own. Of all the great powers France was the most unified, and her own large numbers were the basis of her power. Other states therefore had a reason for adding to their numbers, whether by annexing territory or by promoting economic welfare, and for unifying their peoples in every way that might produce well-knit armies.

Other considerations akin to these, but of even wider scope, affected policy and economic life. Man for man the armies made greater demands on the economy of their countries. When one of them improved its equipment the others had to do as well or better, at their peril. More artillery was needed, more small arms, more ammunition, more transport, greater stores of food, clothing, and boots, to say nothing of more pay and more regular payment. Along with the growth of armies went the rise of the navies. In the sixteenth century specialized ships of war were few in numbers outside the Mediterranean, where the warship was still, as in the times of the Homeric wars, an oared galley, a simple craft, comparatively easy to equip. Naval warfare was largely carried on by armed merchantmen collected from the ports. After Lepanto and the Spanish Armada there was an interval in which there were no large and costly navies anywhere. After that the new Atlantic maritime states began to build up their fleets. The sailing-ship with its broadside of guns dominated the Mediterranean. Merchantmen disappeared from the line of battle. Soon after the middle of the seventeenth century the Dutch and the English began to fight one another with great battle-fleets, and the French tried to emulate their naval standard, just as other powers were trying to reach the French military standard. These fleets could not be fitted out from the home resources of the Atlantic powers. They drew heavily on those resources: naval recruitment was parasitic on the merchant marine; guns, ammunition, clothing, and victualling were needed, as for the armies; but timber was used in quantities which only Norway and the Baltic could supply, and along with it tar and pitch and materials for sailcloth and cordage. To buy and transport these necessaries new financial expedients were required.

Warfare gave the states these urgent reasons for concerning themselves with economic matters at a time when business men were happy to work with the statesmen. Although in well-conducted business a bargain leaves both the buyer and the seller better off than they were before, it was commonly said in those days that one nation's gain was another's loss. When the European traders crowded in to bid against one another as buyers or sellers in the markets of Europe and Asia and America, they often found that the ambassadors were there before them, negotiating for treaties which should give their own countrymen a monopoly or a preference. From time out of mind the regular way of securing a profitable trade had been to buy a monopoly. In every little town there was some guild which enjoyed the sole right to make or to sell this article or that; in every port there were lawful quays where ships had to unload and pay their dues; every state had its trade-barriers, whether it merely laid special charges on foreigners in its own ports or tried to close whole seas, as the Venetians did in the Adriatic, the Danes in Iceland, or the Spaniards in the Pacific. In this again the middle of the seventeenth century seems to have been a new phase. The ending of the great rise in prices was an expression of the ending of the long phase of expansion. Production and transport had overtaken the widening of markets, and it was harder to find new outlets for trade. Competition was more intense. Something might be done by mechanization or by cutting down costs, but the quick way to get an advantage over a rival was to enlist the support of the state against him. Many of the characteristics of economic life at this time followed from the rendering of this support.

First there was protectionism, by which a state restricted certain economic opportunities to its own subjects. In principle it goes back to the beginning of the world, and old trading states like Venice had practised it with many refinements; but, until they attained a measure of internal unity and efficiency, large territorial states were able to use it only in crude and haphazard ways. Its typical instrument is the tariff. In the seventeenth century no state could set up a trade-barrier as impermeable as those of the nineteenth and twentieth. Their hold over society was still imperfect. They usually had to work either through officials who were easily corrupted or through tax-farmers whose interests might run contrary to those of both the state and the trading community. But there was a tendency towards stricter tariffs based on rational, if short-sighted principles. The chief of these was the principle of the balance of trade. This was the idea that the trade of a country should be judged by means of an annual balance-sheet like that of a business. The merchant can tell from his ledger which of his ventures are profitable and which are not, and so the seventeenth-century economists regarded some branches of trade as advantageous and others as detrimental. They favoured most highly those which brought in such goods as they could not supply for themselves, especially the precious metals, in exchange for manufactured articles which employed their labour at home. The colonial trades fulfilled these requirements, while much of the trade within Europe did not. Each country therefore tried to draw up its tariff, and its other protective arrangements such as navigation laws, in such a way as to reserve colonial trade and the other paying trades for its own people, and to confine its own people to these selected channels.

The counterpart of state encouragement was state regulation. The more authoritarian a state was, and the more highly the administrators rated their own understanding of economic affairs, the more they were apt to lay down rules for the conduct of business. Here again they were only continuing, with greater powers and in a wider sphere, activities which had been handed down to them by their predecessors, but they now had the new aim and the new incentive of promoting the unity and strength of their realms. With the new facilities for movement and the new methods of surveying resources, they thought of the whole country as one great farm. The old feudal franchises and local immunities, which they were sweeping away, were objectionable primarily because they enabled rival powers to set themselves up against the state; but often they also impeded the production of wealth. When a nobleman or a municipality levied a toll on river traffic, they interrupted the free movement of goods, and slowed down the concentration of industry in the most promising centres. Governments tried to remove these impediments. The typical statesman of the age was the great French minister Colbert, who was in power from about 1660 to his death in 1683. His successive tariffs were landmarks in the hardening of European protectionism; but he had an even greater task in removing some of the internal tariffs surrounding the old provinces which had been combined to make the French kingdom as he found it. While he was engaged in this negative work of excluding foreign trade and removing domestic obstructions, it was natural that he should also throw his energies into the positive work of increasing industrial production. He issued many regulations which were intended to raise the quality of manufactures, and to provide capital for their expansion.

As it turned out, the paternalism of Colbert had another negative side. Economic enterprise could not be turned into the channels which governments thought desirable except by closing the others, and many French business men would have preferred to take their own risks and make their own mistakes. The time was still far distant when state trading and state management in industry were possible alternatives to private enterprise. Even the manufacture of commodities such as explosives, of which the states were the only large consumers, was mainly in the hands of private firms, and so, when statesmen tried to encourage manufacturers, they commonly acted as imperfectly informed outsiders. The typical form of large-scale enterprise was the joint-stock company to which the state granted a monopoly. It was not an entirely new form but one which had arisen in earlier times when the circumstances called for it; from about the middle of the sixteenth century it was used in the larger business affairs of the English, the Dutch, and the French. In a joint-stock company many shareholders contributed the capital, leaving the management to an inner circle. They brought together far greater accumulations of capital than even the richest merchant would have risked on a single venture, and it was possible for shareholders to come and go without disturbing the continuity of the company's business. There were, of course, special dangers from fraud and mismanagement; but the system took root. In England the aristocracy, and even the kings and queens, took advantage of it to invest in colonial and industrial undertakings. In Holland, where the business class almost coincided with the governing class, several great companies were formed for the purpose of that colonial commerce which was indistinguishable from war against Spain. The Dutch East India Company, the greatest trading concern of seventeenth-century Europe, became almost an imperial power. In France, where the royal authority was more pervasive than in either of these countries, joint-stock companies were created in pursuance of Colbert's policy; but it was their misfortune never to outgrow this tutelage.

Financial institutions changed in consonance with these and other changes of the times. The political decline of Spain was associated with the breakdown of the international finance by which war and diplomacy had been floated. The great banking families were unable to satisfy the demands of the states; the Spanish kings and some others fell far short of the reliability by which alone a borrower can keep his banker as an ally. Each stage in the military and political decline of Spain was signalized by a repudiation of public debts. At the end of the sixteenth century and in the early seventeenth none of the greater western European states was financially sound, and when a new system arose it was unlike the old. States borrowed from abroad even more heavily than before, but among the lenders there were now states and banks which were more or less directly upheld by states. Private finance was connected with public finance. The Dutch, who were pioneers in many fields of business, built up a sound banking system of their own, and Amsterdam became the great money-market of the seventeenth century. Towards the end of the century London originated methods suitable for English conditions, and the eighteenth century was not far advanced when London, although still a centre of borrowing while Amsterdam was the centre of lending, became a rival for the first place in the world of finance.

The theory and practice of economics in this age, of which Colbert gave the classical expression, are often summed up under the name of 'mercantilism' or the 'mercantile system', words which have been understood in many senses, but which almost always cover a close association of political and economic factors. The states aimed at increasing their power through economic prosperity. At home they tried to exorcize discontent and disunion by a policy of welfare. One means of doing this was to remove internal restraints and obstructions to trade, another to stimulate production; but foreign trade seemed to offer the greatest chances of enrichment and the greatest markets for home manufactures, so that a strong state moulded its own country by pressing against the resistance of the surrounding states. This has been well called the economic aspect of sovereignty. The rise of the sovereign states, through the two-sided process of overcoming rival authorities within their realms and eliminating the interference or jurisdiction of external powers, coincided at many points with paternal government and the jealousy of trade. These truths, however, are often overstated. In practice, policy always fell short of its professions, and the picture of western civilization in its economic aspects was still full of variety and confusion. Hardly any of the current generalizations about mercantilism hold good of the greatest trading nation of the time, the Dutch. Among them the commercial interest was so strong and the state so little centralized that almost any profitable opening for business could be followed without the sanction of any co-ordinating body. Again, in many countries there were forces at work in economic life which ran directly counter to the unifying tendencies.

The increase of wealth through commerce implied, or rather was, an increase of all those activities which were carried on by bargaining, by money-transactions, by exchange based on quantitative calculations of profit. It meant a diminution of all the activities which were regulated by custom, tradition, and authority, a movement from status to contract. In the fifteenth century a large proportion of the inhabitants of Europe hardly handled any money at all. A peasant, for instance, might hold his inherited house and farm without paying rent but by working on his lord's land; he might have the right to collect fuel in his lord's woods; he might pay the miller who ground his corn with a proportion of the corn; he would contribute to the Church by giving tithes of his produce. By the end of the seventeenth century a large proportion of the population, especially the urban population of England, Holland, and France, was living by income-economy. The head of each household planned his work with the primary aim of making a money-income, and he spent most of this income as and when he pleased. His discretion in getting and spending had limits, for he had to pay taxes to the state in cash, and he had legal or moral responsibilities to his family, and perhaps to his employees, but, with some such exceptions as these, income-economy meant freedom. Where a large proportion of people in a prosperous community was free to choose whether to save or to spend, and what to invest in or to spend on, the aggregate result of their individual preferences was an independent determinant of economic life. It might build up trades or industries which the statesmen and economists had never thought about, or even disapproved and feared; it might suck away the nourishment from those they tried to promote. So the mercantile system, in so far as there was such a thing, could never make a national economy work like a well-drilled regiment with no will except the word of command.

In practice mercantilism was hampered all round by the traditional obstacles to which it was consciously opposed, and also by these new accompaniments of economic growth. There was no field in which it achieved so little as in the welfare of the peasants and wage-earners. Popular discontent became less alarming to governments in proportion as they got the better of the feudal or municipal powers which might make use of it in armed revolt. Whenever bad times or flagrant injustices caused intolerable poverty, or political confusion inflamed the eternal grievances of the oppressed, there were peasants' risings and journeymen's riots; but, on the whole, they were put down more easily in the seventeenth century than in the sixteenth and more easily in the later seventeenth century than in the earlier. There was a specially disturbed period round the middle of the seventeenth century in such widely different environments as those of England, Bohemia, and Switzerland; and it is to be accounted for on both political and economic, local and general grounds. For similarly complex reasons the late seventeenth century ushered in a more orderly period which lasted through most of the eighteenth. Governments, however, still had the fear of rebellion always in their minds, and, quite apart from that, they had enough sense to see that it was in every way best for the people to be healthy and satisfied. Humanitarian feeling was not impotent. Much was done in the richer countries by private and public charity for the unemployed, the sick, and the orphans. While there were occasionally bitter complaints against the established order of ranks and government it was neither shaken nor seriously criticized. When large numbers of industrial workers were congregated in towns there were tumultuous strikes, and among the more prosperous artisans there were beginnings of something like trade unionism; but they were only beginnings, and they cannot be said to have modified the general position of the workers. In no country was there anything resembling a national working-class movement. Manual workers in different trades had no consciousness of common interests and no network of communication among themselves. It was only in political or religious movements that they acted together over wide areas. Mercantilist thinkers, indeed, for the most part believed that national industry would thrive best if labour was cheap. If civil war and social unrest played a smaller part after the middle of the seventeenth century than before, this came about not as the reward of a policy of welfare, but partly because the states were stronger and better able to keep order, and partly because unguided economic processes carried some share of the new wealth to every stratum of society.

As in its other aspects, sovereignty in its economic aspect gathered, about a few great centres, power which had been dispersed among many that were smaller, and so simplified the scheme of European conflicts. Of this the most notable instance was that of the colonial conflicts. The Portuguese and the Spaniards, as we have seen, built up their trade and their empires under royal auspices and royal regulations; but the newer colonizing nations had far looser relations to their governments. The English Queen Elizabeth gave commissions authorizing her merchant captains to carry on hostilities; and she took shares in the companies which financed them. Her ministers and those of her successor watched their actions closely, and gave diplomatic support when they claimed the right to trade or colonize where the Spaniards had no effective occupation. They gave the highest diplomatic rank to representatives in Turkey and India who were appointed and paid by trading companies. But they regarded trade itself as a matter for companies or merchants and not a matter of state; they neither prescribed rules for its management nor took the initiative in clearing away the barriers set up against it by foreign governments. Some of the most successful of the English colonists owed scarcely anything to official support. New England was founded by religious refugees, whose royal charters in effect merely gave them permission to go their way unmolested. The French and Dutch governments stood in different relations to private enterprise, but their colonists also were far more free from supervision than their fellow subjects who remained at home. None of these three governments therefore espoused the quarrels of its merchants and settlers unless with cause shown. Their European affairs, which involved the issues of war and invasion, were much more important to them than colonial affairs, and colonial affairs soon generated a rivalry of all against all among the trading companies, which could not have been transferred to Europe without ending in anarchy.

Thus it was that in the first half of the seventeenth century there were informal wars in the colonial world which did not bring European wars in their train, because the European governments were not committed to them. When England and Spain were at peace, it was still a maxim of the English sea-rovers that there was no peace beyond the line. When the English attempted to trade with the Spice Islands the Dutch kept them out by violence. Dutch and English whale-fishers fought in the Arctic. There was fierce Anglo-Dutch rivalry wherever the English tried to trade, and the governments supplied their countrymen with munitions and much more. This rivalry led to a long series of diplomatic negotiations, but, all through the period of the Thirty Years War, friendship between the two states was a necessity, so that none of these negotiations ended with an ultimatum. When the Portuguese began their war of independence they almost automatically became allies of the French against the Spaniards; but this was no reason why the Dutch should discontinue their efforts to conquer Brazil, and they still fought against the Portuguese there, though indirectly, as allies of the French, they fought for them in Europe.

There were similar occurrences, though on a small scale and in out-of-the-way places, in later times. In the late seventeenth century, for instance, during a phase of friendship between France and England, the French officials in Canada did more than connive at the capture and destruction of the British trading posts on Hudson Bay. But this was now an exception, and the general rule had altered. About the middle of the century the new colonial states had gained so much in strength, their supervision of colonial trade was so much more strict and jealous, and the affairs of the world were so much more closely knit, that there could no longer be hostilities round the circumference and peace at the centre. First the quarrel of the Dutch and the English came to a head in a regular war in their home waters. This war had other contributing causes, but rivalry in the seas and the Indies was by far the chief. A few years later the Dutch and the Portuguese were openly at war. The French, who regretted this division among the old enemies of Spain, persuaded them to compose their differences; and in the same way, when Anglo-Dutch rivalry led to two more wars within a generation of the first, the quarrel was broken off before it was fought out, because a European danger, this time from France herself, appeared to both the combatants more alarming than anything they had to fear from one another. These nearer and greater dangers in Europe still outweighed all overseas affairs; but the political relations of Europe and the outer world were permanently altered. Henceforward European governments were fully committed to colonial quarrels, and these were a permanent element in the causes of European wars.

For this reason, and for others which necessarily followed from the conditions of the time and from mercantilist policy, each of the great wars in the second half of the century had an economic prelude. Plenipotentiaries were briefed with commercial statistics, and several of the great peace-settlements included treaties which stipulated for modifications of tariffs. There were also new formulae in diplomatic documents, which seemed to imply a more rational ordering of international affairs. The balance of power, or equilibrium of Europe, seemed as much a scientific conception as the balance of trade, and more conducive to the general interest. It was elaborated, by the

Frenchman Sully who had stood in the first rank of statesmen, into a project for maintaining permanent peace between the European states. Their territories were to be so arranged that it could never be to the advantage of any to be an aggressor, and they were to form a federation which should make war on the enemies of Christendom, notably the Turks. The significance of this project, and of the few other proposals for perpetual peace to which the period gave birth, is only that they showed a desire for a better international order, and a belief, or perhaps only a hope or a wish, that policy could end the endemic warfare of Europe. In practice none of these plans had the smallest influence. Nor indeed did the idea of the balance of power provide more than a formula for common action which the states would in any event have taken when they were threatened with aggression, or when they had to agree on some division of territory among themselves. Fundamentally international relations became neither more co-operative nor more scientific.

Some historians have laid the blame for this on one man, King Louis XIV, who ruled over France for more than fifty years exactly at the time when the ascendancy of France over the mind of Europe was at its highest. The French language became not only the language of almost all diplomacy but also the international language of the educated classes, and it began to take the place of Latin as a medium of learned intercourse. French literature reached a classical perfection. The tragedies of Racine and the comedies of Molière became the possession and the models of all Europe. Louis was a great master of pageantry, and Versailles, which he created, became the pattern of royal courts. France set the fashions in dress. The French Academy, and the bodies of lower standing for the specialized sciences, earned high prestige. Yet in many respects the France of Louis XIV was old-fashioned and untouched by the dawning enlightenment. There was a severe censorship of publications. Not only was France outside the movement towards toleration; the Huguenots were even deprived of the toleration which they had enjoyed. They had given no offence and there was no political danger from them; but Louis subjected them to pressure from the beginning of his personal rule. First propaganda and then persecution were used to convert them; they began to emigrate, to the great advantage of the Protestant countries which received them; and finally the Edict of Nantes was repealed. In all these oppressive measures Louis was immediately concerned.

His personality counted for much. He was Spanish on his mother's side, and his religious policy savoured of Spain not only in relation to the Huguenots but in other ways as well. He did not shrink from quarrelling with the Holy See on behalf of the autonomy of the Gallican Church, in which he had so much power. He threw his influence on the side of the Jesuits in a bitter controversy against Jansenism, an evangelical movement with something like a tang of Protestantism in it. In this he did not carry all legal and ecclesiastical France with him, and the controversy outlasted his life-time. But, although he was more than a figurehead, the character of the French state, his own part in it, and its international action sprang from causes far deeper and wider than one man's mind. The events of Louis's early years confirmed the lessons which had already made France choose authoritarian government. During his minority there was anarchy. The old elements of disruption, the nobles and the law-courts, made a bid for power. They lacked the political experience and the social generosity which could have led to a liberal revolution, and an able minister, the Italian Cardinal Mazarin, restored his own authority and the king's by methods more adroit and less drastic than those of Richelieu. It was not until the defeats of Louis's later years that opposition again raised its head. Then some of its leaders used the true language of liberalism; but they had no programme except government by a narrow aristocratic class which was unfit for the burden. The nobility existed and could not be ignored, but as a body it was politically useless. Some of its members were content with the harmless occupations of courtiers, and many more took up the career which the French army, like the other professional armies of the time, afforded.

Absolutism was the only method by which France could be kept in order and maintain her inherited international pretensions. More than that, it was a system of government which could boast genuine successes. It provided Colbert with the administrative machinery that he needed. One of his fellow ministers brought the army into a better state of discipline and into stricter subordination to the state than it had ever known before. The great departments which could do so much could only work in accordance with their own construction, and Louis could not arbitrarily change the interaction of their parts. As the state ceased to be feudal it became impersonal. The king did not read all the documents that he signed, let alone write them. He even used secretaries who were authorized to forge his autograph. He did not understand all the decisions that he announced, let alone form them. By his time France, and others of the larger states, were passing into the condition, known in our day as that of all states and of some great private organizations, in which few men in office have actual power as extensive as their nominal responsibility. In such a state of things to talk of a policy as that of one man is seldom more than a picturesque abbreviation.

9

Sixty Years of Warfare, 1659–1721

WHEN EUROPE WAS half-pacified by the treaty of the Pyrenees in 1659 the two main facts of the situation were that Spain was declining apace and that France had become the strongest of the powers. France laid claim to the gratitude of states, such as the Dutch republic and those of the German princes, which she had saved from Spanish or Austrian Habsburg domination. She had ties of friendship with a ring of states, Sweden, Poland, and Hungary, which had helped her to encircle the Habsburgs. She had a party at her service in every capital, as the Spaniards had once had in the days of her greatness. She had agents in every discontented province. While the economic and political drift was towards intensified international competition, she had all the assets which could be of use in warfare. France had already passed from defence to attack, and for nearly fifty years she was never at war except of her own choice. She had the political initiative, and her opponents could not choose whether or when or where to begin hostilities or how to end them. The king and his people revelled in their glory. A few men whose voices could be heard in high places stigmatized the wars as cruel and unjust. They were easily silenced, and, so long as the victories lasted, they were forgotten.

The greatest issue in all these wars was the future of the Spanish dominions. They were still by far the richest and most populous which were owned by any European state, but Spain would certainly not be able to hold them together. Soon after Louis began his personal rule, a prospect came in sight which made it appear a public duty for France to control the settlement of this issue. The Spanish throne fell to a pitiable weakling who had no heir and no prospect of an heir. His death would bring into operation the old insurance system of the Habsburgs, by which the Austrians were to inherit if the Spanish line came to an end. This would have renewed the danger to France from Habsburg encirclement. Forty years went by before this fateful death occurred, and during these forty years the stakes became steadily higher. International relations went through the changes we have noticed in the last chapter, and France, under Colbert, had the initiative here too. In Canada the settlers and traders became pioneers of empire; the city of St. Louis was founded on the Mississippi, and it was possible to travel in French territory from the mouth of the St. Lawrence to the Gulf of Mexico. In Europe Colbert created a navy which made France a third maritime power on the Atlantic. If such a France were victorious over Spain the whole western and colonial world might well be at her mercy.

There were nearly thirty years of French aggrandizement before the grouping of the European powers fell into conformity with these threatening realities. On his northern and eastern and southern frontiers Louis edged forwards, taking one province and one fortress after another from Spain or from the empire in open war, or in undeclared war, or by ostensibly legal processes which had the threat of war behind them. But during that generation there were other European states which half-consciously prepared for a struggle. Some of the German princes resented the dominance which France had acquired on the pretext of protecting them against the Habsburgs. There were Austrian diplomatists everywhere who exposed the fallacies of the Francophil arguments. The Dutch held out stubbornly for their rights in the Baltic, and took alarm at the French advance to the south of them in the Spanish Netherlands. For a time Dutch policy was perplexed by the continuing British rivalry. The English strengthened their Portuguese alliance. Portugal was able to save Brazil and, after handing over strategic bases to the English, she saved all the other parts of her empire which the Dutch had not already seized. In the second of the Anglo-Dutch wars the new French navy was nominally on the Dutch side, but the English made valuable colonial gains at the expense of the Dutch. They took New Netherland, renamed New York, so connecting New England with Virginia and their more recent settlements in Maryland and Carolina. They gave up, however, their hopes of ousting the Dutch from the richest parts of the Malay Archipelago, and, though there was another war, in which the British and French navies co-operated while the French invaded Holland, the very success of this French invasion caused the English and the Dutch to suspend their colonial strife. It seemed a miracle that the Dutch were able to summon Spanish, imperial and Protestant German help and to save their independence. For ten more years France still divided and browbeat her neighbours; but at last another miracle happened. William III of Orange, the great-grandson of William the Silent, more than any other man, or any hundred other men, had saved his country in the hour of invasion. England had a revolutionary crisis in its religious and constitutional affairs, and the opponents of France, of Catholic emancipation, and of authoritarian government needed a leader. The irony of fate gave them their leader by the working of the ancient dynastic principle, for William and his wife had a place, though not the first place, in the line of succession to the English crown. The opposition summoned him to England and to the throne. He saved western Europe, as he had saved Holland, by bringing Spain, the emperor, German princes, and yet other allies into the field, while at last the Dutch and the British fleets held the seas in concert.

There was an indecisive war of nine years (1688–97). It was a European war, involving all the continent except the east and the Baltic; indeed it was a world war. It was followed by a peace of four years in which all parties sincerely tried to overcome their mutual suspicions and reach agreement on the specific questions, territorial and economic, over which war might arise; but it was not only disagreements about 'danger-spots' that divided them. The world was now so closely knit that every local question ran into every other, and the contest for power embraced them all. Finally the crisis of the Spanish inheritance broke. Well-intentioned statesmen in every country searched for some compromise which should satisfy all the parties. It seemed that this first world-empire could be liquidated by partition. One accident after another dissipated all such hopes, and at last the Spaniards themselves made all compromise impossible by insisting that their empire should be kept together as a single whole. The method they chose was to offer it not, it is true, to France, but to a younger line of the French royal house. That decision brought the armies and the fleet of King Louis to their side, but in the new world war, which lasted for fourteen years, the victory was not theirs. The principle of partition was applied after all, and France was forced back from some of her advanced positions.

These sixty years of warfare changed the map of western and Mediterranean Europe. They left France territorially larger than she had been before, with fresh provinces on the Pyrenees and on the eastern frontier and with parts of provinces torn away from the Netherlands. She had become strategically not less but more compact. The wars left the Dutch republic financially exhausted, and politically checked. They left Spain a second-class power, still mistress of the Indies but no longer of the Netherlands, or Milan, or Sicily. It was now Austria which undertook the task of defending all these three, and they gave her a great accession of strength, though of strength outside Germany. The old combination of the Spanish and Austrian Habsburgs was ended after its two troubled centuries of validity and Spain became normally a client state of France. Germany had become a theatre of rival ambitions. Brandenburg-Prussia had come forward into the front rank of German states. Its electors of the house of Hohenzollern had been both crafty and lucky in earning payments for their alliance. They had imitated the military organization and the conscription of the Swedes to such purpose that they had beaten Swedish troops in the field. They had adopted French methods with equal success, and they had begun to build up their own capable and heavy-handed bureaucratic state. The emperor had raised them to royal rank. Two other German electors had reached the same elevation. An elector of Hanover had succeeded to the British crown as the Protestant nominee, and the elector of Saxony had become a Catholic and had been elected by Austrian influence as King of Poland. Thus in Germany all was ready for future contests.

For Europe generally the problem of French power was not ended, but it had entered a new phase. Spain was no longer the chief antagonist. Opposition now looked to the threefold combination of Austria, Great Britain, and the Dutch, which had an experience of common action matching its common interests. Now that the stronger states were more consolidated, and had welded together their colonial and economic affairs with their home affairs, their mutual relations were more orderly. The successive coalitions against Louis XIV were based on compromise between the general interest in the balance of power and the cupidities of separate states; but they were less impudently rapacious than the alliances of the fifteenth and sixteenth centuries. They had some conception of a common good of Europe, and both sides accepted the principle of equilibrium as the ostensible basis of treaties of peace. In conducting their wars, the states of the coalitions had gained great experience of international co-operation, experience from which the technique and the spirit of diplomacy ultimately benefited everywhere. They had worked together not only to win and divide the spoils of victory, but also to save their power of managing their own affairs, and this effort had made them move, some farther and others less far, some unconsciously and others to the accompaniment of economic and political theorizing, towards the conception of the state not as dynastic property but as the guardian of the welfare of the land.

As an effective force in affairs this conception still took for granted the social fabric of limited governing classes ruling over an unenfranchized population. In no western country, and not even in any of the colonial settlements, was there any true democracy, any manhood suffrage or even any serious demand for it. But, while this period saw the extinction of this revolutionary challenge, it saw what may be called aristocratic or oligarchic liberalism established in a new stronghold. Aristocratic liberalism was government in accordance with the agreed decisions of bodies which were drawn from a limited class but acted after free discussion and with some degree of tolerance and of consideration for the governed. Its germs were alive in the estates constitutions of the Middle Ages. They had survived in more places than one through the period when despotism carried all before it in most of the continental countries. Hungary, for instance, still had its parliament, and there were one or two minor German principalities where the estates counted for something. Only one of the greater powers, the Dutch republic, however, had always managed its business on these lines, and it was a fact of the greatest moment that, at the time when this first sponsor of modern freedom was losing its place in the front rank, another state, of which the prospects had for long seemed uncertain, stood forward indubitably as a great European power and a liberal state.

This was Great Britain. Before the accession of King William III she had never been free from ecclesiastical and constitutional divisions. Richelieu, Mazarin, and Louis XIV had each played on these divisions, which kept England out of the European field; but the island was never invaded. The governing class worked out its own solution for its problems, the solution of a constitutional monarchy, co-operating with Parliament and granting toleration, but not full civil rights, to religious dissidents. William III was equally the representative of this settlement and of an active resistance to France in Europe and overseas. In his time Great Britain began to act as the equal of Austria in the European coalitions. Her fleets were larger than those of the Dutch. After William's time her land-armies were directed by the genius of Marlborough, and in the peace-settlement she gained colonial conquests in Newfoundland and Nova Scotia, and also strategic positions in Gibraltar and Minorca. It was her liberalism which enabled her to deploy so much of her strength. She turned the personal union of England and Scotland into a constitutional union on a parliamentary basis. She modernized her finances by a close association between Parliament and the business world. And this was the time in which the steam-engine was invented and the fame of Newton spread abroad. For the first time since the early sixteenth century there were English thinkers among the recognized leaders of European thought. English imaginative literature in its great days from Shakespeare to Milton had been the private and untranslated possession of the islanders; but now Europe and even France began to learn from English teachers. Newton's contemporary Locke wrote the classics of liberalism. He wrote as a Christian and an Anglican, but he wrote in terms which exactly suited the fashionable demand for reasonableness in all things. He advocated toleration, within limits; he defended the bloodless revolution which had brought in William III; he argued that good government must be government by consent, and that the ultimate guarantee against arbitrary rule was to preserve society by revolution in the state. He wrote much else, about theology and philosophy and education and economics, and he played his part in public affairs; but it was as a political theorist that he made his mark on history. There were continental and American readers for a century after his time, some of them sparing no attention for his ambiguities and reservations, who followed him in believing that the powers of governments ought to be limited by law, and that laws ought to be made by bodies chosen by the citizens.

The measure of the growing strength of western civilization in the time of Louis XIV is the reversal of the old relations with the Turks. For the first twenty years of Louis's time the divisions of the west still prevented any strong action against them. There was even a renewal of Turkish vigour and efficiency. After they had crushed the Persian revival the Turks turned westwards again and attacked the Venetians in Crete. Then, indeed, there was an episode which promised great things for the future. The emperor picked a quarrel with the Turks, and in 1663, at the abbey of St. Gothard on the river Raab in Hungary, he inflicted on them their first land-defeat in Europe. But this promise, like the promise of Lepanto, was not fulfilled. Louis XIV had sent a small contingent to share in the triumph; but he did not take up the Turkish war in earnest. The emperor had to make a truce, and French ambition in the west diverted his energies so effectively that he kept it for eighteen years. The Turks took Crete. They supported the rebellious Cossacks of the Ukraine against the Poles and they took the fertile province of Podolia for themselves. There was nothing to show that this would be their last considerable gain of European land. There was nothing to cause them apprehension in the advance of the Russians, with Cossack aid, along the Dnieper. Austria, the main enemy, was weakened by long wars against France; the Turks attacked again in Hungary, and in 1683 once more, as in 1529, they reached Vienna. This time they besieged it, and for two months it was in peril. It was saved when John Sobieski, the King of Poland, led his gallant cavalry charge.

With the deliverance of Vienna a new era began in eastern Europe. Louis could never command sufficient strength there to turn the traditional friendship to the advantage of either France or the Turks: from Algiers to the Aegean, as he weakened, the Turks were weakened too. At last Austria, Poland, and Venice in alliance fought a long war, and the results were marvellous. Although the emperor had to fight on two fronts throughout the Nine Years War against France he and his allies defeated the Turks again and again. In 1699, at Carlowitz, peace was made. For the first time the Turks agreed to a treaty in a conference where mediators, British and Dutch, presided. Its terms registered the end of the Turkish danger. Venice regained the Morea. The Poles recovered Podolia. The Habsburgs took Transylvania and almost the whole plain of Hungary. This was the first stage in the expulsion of the Turks from Europe. It was still to take two centuries before they were expelled from the rest of the continent; even now they are in Istanbul; and it was long before Hungary was recolonized and politically settled, but the Turkish occupation had left nothing behind it that could serve as a foundation for their return.

This first advance showed how great a material and moral superiority western civilization had wrung from its conflicts in the centuries since the invention of printing. It was followed by a few years in which the Habsburgs were drawn off into the last war against Louis XIV, while Hungary rose in a national rebellion behind them and other powers fought confusedly in the Ukraine; but once Louis was brought to terms, the Austrian armies again moved down the Danube, and the treaty of Passarowitz in 1718 marked the second stage in the Turkish evacuation. Venice, indeed, lost the Morea. Greece remained in subjection for a century more, and the career of the Venetian republic as a power was ended. But the dominions of the Habsburgs had reached their largest extent. Belgrade was once more a Christian town, and they ruled a great part of Serbia. From Vienna they set themselves to organize, to subject and, as far as might be, to unify peoples who spoke ten or a dozen languages and lived at every level of civilization from that of a polished capital to that of a devastated frontier. Neither in religious toleration nor in constitutional liberalism had they learnt anything whatsoever from the example of the western states or from the experience of their own subjects.

Since the fifteenth century the western state-system had broadened to include all Europe from the Hebrides to the Dardanelles; but from the frontier of Norway to the Caspian were states which moved in their own orbits, chiefly absorbed in questions of little moment to the Atlantic and Mediterranean powers. England, France, and Holland, it is true, had their economic concern with the Baltic; the Turks and Austrians had to watch Russia and Poland, and none of these states could be indifferent to the affairs of the north and north-east; but in the middle of the seventeenth century observers in the west were accustomed to thinking of the Baltic states, Denmark, Sweden, and Poland, as forming, with some of their German neighbours and Russia, a separate northern system regulated by its own balance of power. The northern system was perpetually agitated by wars, but here the armies were smaller, there were few strongly held lines of fortifications, and so the campaigns ranged over greater distances. In this period the wars led to several decisive results. One after another the three leading Baltic powers exhausted their energies until they fell back into the second rank, among the states which relied for their preservation not on their own strength but on allies or patrons.

The Swedes had two more great soldier-kings after Gustavus Adolphus. The first of these, Charles Gustavus, had something of the same reputation as a Protestant hero; but his successes were gained at the expense of Protestant Denmark. He drove the Danes out of their remaining provinces on the Swedish side of the straits which separated the two kingdoms. Temporarily he conquered another province, which brought him to the sea-coast of Norway, but the permanent result of his wars was to give Sweden the boundaries which it has today. His successor combined with the peasantry against the nobles to establish an absolute monarchy. From his time, however, the Swedish empire was on the defensive. The Swedes had not only the Danes against them, but from time to time the Dutch, who feared for their Baltic trade, and the Brandenburgers, who feared for their access to the sea. The French, as of old, supported the Swedes, and so their empire held together for a time; but their resources were insufficient to defend the long land perimeter and their sea-power was insufficient to maintain their communications. In 1699 the fourth king of the house of Vasa, Charles XII, had to face a coalition of aggressors. For twenty-two years the Great Northern War, as it was called, rolled backwards and forwards from Copenhagen to Estonia and the Ukraine. Charles XII was a heroic figure, at once determined to maintain his country's territories and blind to its sufferings; but he was also a scientific soldier of great ability. He fought the Danes, the Poles, the Russians. He never surrendered; he never made a definitive peace; but it is also true that his terms, when he was victorious, were always moderate, and that he was never the aggressor. Three years after his death in action, Sweden made peace and paid a heavy price. Brandenburg-Prussia took one part of the Baltic coast, and Russia far more. In the eighteenth century there were Swedes who rose to European reputation in the arts and sciences, and the kings lived grandly, but, except for Sweden and Finland, their possessions, a few unimportant German districts, were held on sufferance.

Denmark gained nothing of moment from all this. There too absolute monarchy was established; but Denmark remained an agricultural country politically in the second rank. Poland fell with Sweden. Charles Gustavus took Warsaw and Cracow, and he planned a partition of Poland. The Danes and Austrians prevented this; but the Poles had to renounce their claims on Sweden and Livonia, and their overlordship over East Prussia. Much greater losses soon followed. After a war of thirteen years the Poles abandoned their ambitions in the direction of Russia, leaving Smolensk for good. Kiev also they handed over: the surrender was meant to be temporary, but it too was lasting. The Ukrainian Cossacks on the left bank of the Dniester had passed from Polish to Russian suzerainty. There followed a period of peace with Russia in which the Poles did good service against the Turks, service from which in the end not they but the Austrians reaped the advantage. They recovered some lost territory by the Treaty of Carlowitz; but they were weakening. In the same year the elector of Brandenburg acquired their port of Elbing. Above all the internal condition of Poland was going from bad to worse. The elections of the kings were dominated by foreign powers: French candidates were put up against Austrian candidates. The authority of the crown sank lower than ever. The gentry were still highly civilized, but neither they nor the magnates showed political sense. The Jesuits completely controlled education and the old toleration was ended: in 1658 the anti-Trinitarians were banished. Charles XII made short work of the Polish armies. Like Charles Gustavus he occupied both Warsaw and Cracow. When he was defeated by the Russians at Poltava in 1709 they, without making war on Poland, were able to exert a preponderating influence in Polish affairs. The king, Augustus the Strong, elector of Saxony, who was restored after an interlude of a French-sponsored king of Polish stock, had originally been put in by the Austrians; but now he reigned as a Russian puppet. Poland, like the outlying Swedish provinces, survived on sufferance. The idea of partitioning it was becoming familiar. At one time or another the Russians, the Austrians, the Brandenburgers, and Augustus the Strong himself, all suggested it; the diplomatists of other powers speculated anxiously as to whether they were in earnest.

The Baltic, the Ukraine, and Poland were now all dominated by Russia from the east; but this was much more than a shifting of the balance of power between the states of this system. It was a revolution in the relations between the eastern and the western-central civilizations. The west had been transformed intellectually and materially; consequently the western question had been transformed for the Russians. As trade grew and diplomatic missions became more frequent, as one Scottish officer and one German physician after another came to seek his fortune, knowledge of the west accumulated. There had been printing in Moscow since the second half of the sixteenth century. It had scarcely been used except for ecclesiastical purposes; but some of the leading men of the country imported books of every kind. About the middle of the seventeenth century, however, it seems that foreign influence had done less to modify Russian ways than to excite repugnance. Even among reformers and innovators there were some whose inspiration was entirely homebred. In 1649 the Tsar Alexis brought in a code of laws which is said to have taken something away from the powers of the monarchy, and so to have been contrary in spirit to the contemporary tendency of legislation in the western countries.

The first great changes in Russian life which resulted from contact with the west were in the ecclesiastical sphere. In 1650 two scholars of Kiev were called to Moscow to translate the Bible into Russian. This must be regarded as a following of western examples, though not of any one example in particular. The western influence was even less specific, though equally operative, in the innovations introduced, with far-reaching consequences for the future, by the patriarch Nikon. He asserted the independence of the Church from lay control and even claimed that it was superior to the royal authority. In this Tsar Alexis defeated him; but he introduced ecclesiastical reforms which showed, both in their own substance and in the reactions which they provoked, how utterly Russian Orthodoxy differed from either Roman Catholicism or Protestantism, and how utterly the Russian people differed from the peoples of the west.

The reforms themselves dealt with matters which were small, but to describe them as trivial is to betray ignorance both of history and of human nature. Nikon made some corrections in the text of the Bible and of service-books. He altered some points of ritual, such as the position of the fingers in giving the blessing. It would not be difficult to mention instances of even smaller changes which were bitterly contested in the west. Less than a century earlier, for instance, the Capuchin reform of the Franciscan Order had turned on a change in the cut of the friars' hoods. Small things are not trivial if they are symbolic, and many of the lower clergy regarded Nikon's innovations as symbols. He followed the best Greek manuscripts and practices; but in Constantinople the Church, besides being Greek, not Russian, was open to western influences. A generation earlier a patriarch there had corresponded with Anglican and Protestant divines, and his reforming dreams had ended with his murder. It is scarcely surprising that Nikon's opponents thought he was polluting Russian Christianity with Greek innovations and Romish heresies. Nor does its emotional intensity make their resistance different in kind from the schisms of the west. The difference is that in Russia there was a sectarian movement which owed nothing, even at a distant remove, to leaders of thought, but everything to instinctive dread of what was foreign and unfamiliar.

Those who refused to conform were persecuted. They persisted with fanatical determination, and they survived as sects under the name of Old Believers. These bodies, consisting mostly of peasants and traders, were strong among the colonists of the frontiers. They thought of the power of the state as a tyranny, an evil. Their schism, like the Lutheran Reformation in the west, was the signal for the rise of many other sects, evangelical, mystical, or extravagant, and Russia for the first time had its spiritual revolutionaries. On its side the Orthodox Church ceased to be equivalent to the people in its religious aspect; it became a body in alliance with the state and the educated class. Its leaders took sides for or against welcoming western influences; and when Russia pushed forward into the 'western lands' this division in high places became more momentous. Many of the new subjects of the tsar in the Ukraine were well acquainted with Polish manners and letters. For some forty years before Tsar Alexis annexed it, Kiev had been the most active intellectual centre of the Orthodox Church. It was no small matter that this tsar had three of his children taught the Polish and Latin languages.

Thus far the western question had unsettled Russia. By the end of the seventeenth century it came to a crisis. Russian expansion was going forward in the old slow, many-headed way. In 1662 there were probably no more than 70,000 Russians in Siberia; in 1710 there were probably considerably more than 330,000, something like the same number as the British colonists in North America. They had a stable frontier, fixed by a treaty with China in 1689, along the Argun river. The advance in the Ukraine brought the Russians into the front line of the war with the Turks: as we have seen, they were in alliance with the Austrians in their war on the Danube, and before the first cessation of that war they captured Azov. The Russians were not parties to the treaty of Carlowitz, but their representatives took part in the negotiations, and so won recognition as members of the same state-system with the west. As their state grew in strength, and as success nourished its territorial ambitions, the Russians saw the technical and intellectual superiority of the west at closer quarters. Then a direct western threat to their safety brought the crisis. The Swedes and the Turks made an alliance against them. The Russians went into the Great Northern War with the hope of winning some of the Baltic provinces from Sweden. Charles XII, who had needed the support of the Dutch fleet to get the better of the Danes, routed the Russian army single-handed and easily. It was unequal to war against the western states. From that hour the whole future of the country turned on the western question.

The tsar who had taken Azov and sent his ambassadors to Carlowitz drew the moral. He was Peter the Great. He used all the powers of his sovereignty, and all the furious strength of his character, to force the western sciences and manners upon Russia; but, although he opened her doors wide to western influences, he did it in order to keep western power at arm's length. He lived only fifty-three years, and his effective rule lasted only from 1694 until his death in 1725.

We have seen already that in the end he worsted Sweden. He deprived her of the Baltic provinces of Ingria, Carelia, Estonia, and Livonia. To him this meant more than an addition of territory and more than the control of the trade-route to the Baltic and the west. It was the beginning of sea-power. He built a fleet on the Baltic, fifty ships of the line, carrying 20,000 men. He built his new capital Petersburg in the marshes of the River Neva in Ingria. He did not actually use this new European outlet for any further advance. He took some part in European politics, naturally against the French because he was against the Turks and the Swedes, and consequently favouring the Austrians and the maritime powers. But, like Charles XII, he refused to be drawn into the western wars. Even against the Turks he made no headway. At the instigation of Sweden they renewed their war against him and they took Azov away again. After that he fought the Persians in alliance with the Turks, and extended his frontiers on that side. But he had taken the decision to join on equal terms in the contests of the great powers. He increased and modernized and westernized his army. In 1716 he issued a military code on the western model. He had a field army of perhaps 100,000 men, smaller than that of France but of the same order of magnitude as that of Austria, and far larger than those of Sweden or Prussia.

Although he was at war for twenty-eight years Peter carried out great plans of national reorganization. As a young man he learnt much from the German residents in Moscow and from the foreign officers of the army. He studied mathematics, navigation, fortification. He travelled incognito in Germany, Holland, and England, and learnt much of the crafts of shipbuilding, gunnery, anatomy, engraving; and he got an idea of western politics and ecclesiastical affairs. He recruited foreign technicians and officers. He did away with the prohibition on foreign travel for Russians and even compelled some of them to study abroad. He developed economic resources on foreign models, introducing the vine, the mulberry, and tobacco in his south-eastern provinces. He opened mines, and at the end of his time Russia was producing more iron than Great Britain. He projected great public works, to serve both economic and strategic ends: a canal from the Don to the Volga, another from the Volga by Lake Ladoga to the Neva. He transplanted what he could of western enlightenment, and what he transplanted was in the new fashion of the time. He did something for education, especially for technical education. To printing he gave some little encouragement, and he established a newspaper. In 1724 he founded the Russian Academy of Sciences. It was not until three years after his death that a university was founded in Petersburg.

The line which he took in religion was determined by the confusion which had followed the schism. The conservatism of the clergy was an obstacle to his plans; their divisions were a danger. He therefore allowed the patriarchate to remain vacant and to lapse. He confiscated much monastic property. He did nothing to bring together the Orthodox and the western churches, but it was with the advice of a former Uniate, who had studied in Rome and in Lutheran Germany, that he frustrated the plan of the bishops for merging the Russian Church with the Orthodox of other lands and detaching it from the state. Instead of consenting to this, he set up the Holy Synod over it, which was a government department. Thus he perpetuated the division of the Russian nation between the state-Church and the sects, and sharpened the division between the educated few and the suffering many.

Although he tried to westernize even the illiterate masses, for instance by prohibiting the old national dress, he did nothing to raise their status. Economically he even subjected the peasants still more to the land-owners. In several ways he made land-tenure even more than in the past a function of service to the state. Although the social foundations remained the same, they were made to support a political structure of a new design. Finance was reformed by the introduction of a poll-tax. There was a rapid output of legislation, much of it amended and superseded as soon as it was promulgated. The last check on autocratic power, the council of magnates, was done away with. A senate of nine members, later increased in numbers, was charged with legislation. Municipal institutions on a German model were introduced. Government departments were set up, with a board at the head of each, as in several western states of the time, according to a plan drawn up by Leibniz. The country was divided into twelve governorships, with areas which survived as long as the Russian monarchy. Peter drew up a table of fourteen ranks, to one or other of which each of his subjects was assigned. In this wonderfully mechanical grading, birth and office each counted for something; but the interplay between the two was not lubricated, as it was in the west, by the inherent adaptability of the wealthy and the aristocrats, or interrupted as it was in Asia by the uncontrolled caprice of the despot. In Russia the service of the state was a middle term unknown elsewhere.

Many of Peter's reforms were projects rather than achievements.

Very likely he did not improve the economic condition of the country; it is thought that in his time the population declined. He did not make Russia a creative centre of the scientific movement: that, in any case, needed time. The western question in the sphere of the mind was still a question of admitting and receiving western ideas. Although by now the west was learning much from further Asia, Russia transmitted nothing. Peter could do nothing to fuse the spiritual inheritance of his people with that of the west, and scarcely anything to spread enlightenment except in the governing circles. During his reign thousands of pagans around Kazan and the Middle Volga were enticed or bullied into a real or nominal Christianity; but in his territories as a whole Islam made more converts than Christianity and made some from its professed adherents. With all its shortcomings, however, Peter's work helped to shape the lines of the European inheritance from his time to ours. He had let in so much from the west that much more was certain to follow; and he had let it in on such conditions that for a long time to come the Russian monarchy could govern the stream. Russia had become as much a member of the western state-system as Austria or France, and he had shown how western skill could be used to develop Russia without delivering her over to western power or western wealth or western ideas.

10

The Baroque[1]

TOWARDS THE MIDDLE of the sixteenth century, when the impetus of the Renaissance was perhaps slackening already, the social condition of Italy deteriorated, as we saw, and became much less propitious for the arts; but we have also seen that before very long they recovered their vigour, not only in Italy, but in the Netherlands, in Spain, and indeed throughout Europe, wherever there was a breathing-space in this angry time. The arts of the late sixteenth century and the seventeenth did not, however, simply continue those of the Renaissance. The spirit of the Renaissance lived on, and not, like the Gothic, as a survival or a substratum, seen, for the most part, only in popular art. Here and there, as in English church-building, conservative feeling checked the degeneration of medieval forms and maintained them, as a more or less separate style, side by side with the classical; but, even where this was so, their principles were largely forgotten. The seventeenth century did not put the sixteenth behind it nearly so completely. The classical feeling for proportion and moderation, once it was recovered, never disappeared again, nor did the characteristics of classical style in architecture and decoration. This was partly because the classical revival was embodied in printed books and engravings, whereas Gothic art was left behind by the printers along with so much else that was medieval; but it was also

[1] For the sake of brevity this chapter does not deal with the tendency called 'mannerism' which historians of art now usually interpose between the harmonious classical Renaissance and the baroque. It takes its name from a remark of the sixteenth-century historian Vasari, that in his time all artists imitated the manner of Michelangelo. This mannerism continues until El Greco and is found in many places. It expresses passion and tension, and is characterized by elongated human figures, elegance and serpentine curves.

partly because liberal education was based on the classical writers. Although taste often changed its favourites, the range of classical writers was so wide that, down to the time of Louis XIV, new literary movements could always attach themselves to Greek or Latin models. Both in literature and in the arts there were always elements which could not be assimilated into classical treatment; but there were always schools which kept classical purity before them as their standard. From somewhere about the middle of the sixteenth century, however, there formed beside this spirit another, which has also existed ever since, sometimes in new combinations with it, but sometimes in opposition.

This tendency is often called the baroque, a name which has the convenience of being a mere nonsense-word, not professing to imply any analysis of the thing to which it is affixed. The thing is not a period in the general history of the arts, for the baroque, however it may be defined, never became the universal fashion among artists, and in some countries, such as England and even France, it never predominated over the classical. There are indeed French châteaux of which the exterior shows nothing of the baroque and the contemporary interior decoration is entirely given over to it. Nor is it in any strict sense a style, for it constantly rebelled against the limitations and proprieties of conformity to settled style. It is a tendency, or if that is too quiet a word for something essentially robust and demonstrative, a force. One of its characteristics is the desire for effect. Baroque architects aimed at the superlative, at the appeal of mass and spaces, at grandeur. Mere size did not satisfy them; they used every device for magnifying its impressiveness by leading the eye to distances. They disguised the structure of their buildings under loads of ornament and improbable curves, playing with their materials almost as if they were designing scenery for the stage. They made their buildings exciting by contrasts. They lavished gilding and coloured marbles on sculptured pulpits and baldachinos, and they brought the spectacle close to the spectator by naturalistic realism in detail.

In painting Rubens has the same exuberance, and some of the Italian devotional painters are equally theatrical. They throw up the anguished or ecstatic features of their saints by melodramatic stage-lighting. Even Rembrandt, who has none of this emotionalism, is as baroque as they are. He kept a stock of gorgeous costumes for his models, and in his art he touched the two opposite extremes of close observation and of evoking the invisible. There was a change in the modes of seeing which found its fullest expression in some of Rembrandt's pictures, where the composition is disposed not vertically and horizontally but diagonally, where interest is concentrated in the centre, from which an incorporeal light glows outwards, merging objects together so as to show not determinate surfaces or lines, but space in depth. If such a change could ever be fully explained, no doubt a great part of the explanation would lie within the technical history of art; but another part of it would be drawn from all the other fields to which the conception of the baroque can be applied.

As it happens there is scarcely any field to which it has not been applied. It has been given the credit for every kind of ostentation or enjoyment that was popular in the seventeenth century, from periwigs to champagne. In literature it has been used to account for the measureless passions of Shakespeare's tragic heroes. When, however, we are told that the mathematics of the seventeenth century were baroque, we begin to suspect that such a conception can be misused. The argument is that mathematicians were much concerned with infinity, and that they have this in common with the artists who falsified perspective and led the eye beyond finite distances. There were architects who were also mathematicians. The greatest of them, Sir Christopher Wren, was an Englishman, and more than one restraint kept him from exaggeration and from mere display or mere virtuosity; but it can hardly be doubted that his mathematical bent was one of them. Without pretending that the nature of the baroque can be expressed in any formula, we ought to keep our idea of it within bounds, not including anything merely on the evidence of a fortuitous or superficial resemblance.

So regarded, it is easily seen to be connected with some of the great movements of the time. In painting and architecture it began in Rome, and, although its seeds were sown earlier, it flowered as an expression of the Catholic Reformation. The Jesuits had their own decided views about the planning and adornment of their churches. They wanted to make them impressive, and they wanted to drive a message home. There was not, as has sometimes been said, a 'Jesuit style', but the baroque did these things for them, and as religious and ecclesiastical revival spread outwards from Rome, they carried it with them to Spain and Portugal, to Austria, Bavaria, and Poland. Wherever there were artists who pressed beyond the bounds of the technique which they had learnt and wherever there were patrons who craved for the grand and the arresting, something of the baroque appeared; but it was in Catholic countries that it most completely captured ecclesiastical and secular art. The new influences from overseas provided it with decorative motifs, or stage-properties; it took on local forms in different climates and environments; but, all through the period with which we are concerned, in France and the Protestant countries it was more an overflow than a spring. The scientific and rational movement was unfavourable to it, and was closely connected, especially in literature, with a contrary tendency to clearness and simplicity. This tendency grew strong in both prose and poetry towards the end of the seventeenth century, for instance in the French drama and the English novel. It suited the tastes of the widening numbers of readers in the prosperous western countries. It made the 'enlightenment' of the eighteenth century comparatively restrained and sober, and it had its counterpart in the arts in lightness, daintiness, and the preference for the pretty to the ponderous.

Here we may glance at some of the great changes which western civilization had undergone since the fifteenth century. The map of the baroque gives another proof that the medieval unity had partly broken down, but it also shows that the result was not a mere splitting into Catholic and Protestant fragments, but something far more complex. Besides religion other factors of the Middle Ages had lost some of their unifying effect. The universities had increased in number with the growth of population, and served at least as many social needs as before, but they were no longer international to the same degree. Latin was still much used in learned writing and in lecturing, but the vernacular languages were gaining ground. The wandering scholars, teachers, and students were now the exception rather than the rule. States had set up national universities, or put obstacles in the way of attending universities abroad, and some of them had fostered or permitted schools of other types, following a more modern curriculum, and not organized as corporations. In spite of the development of international law and of international intercourse, the legal profession was less international than it had been. In England, for instance, the Roman canon law had been suppressed, and the Roman civil lawyers had been hemmed in to a position of very limited influence by the practitioners of a national system of law.

In these and other ways states and nations had loosened the old unities, and, as we saw, their action had much to do with the religious disruption. There were still states which were not national, and nations which were not under states of their own; but in many places and for many reasons state and nation were drawing together. The dynastic and proprietary system was substantially unshaken, and there was no visible weakening in the social foundation of states in the family and the hierarchy of ranks; but the interminable wars had steadily raised the demands which armaments and the rest of the apparatus of power made on social organization. One new state, the Dutch republic, had been born. Some states of the second stratum in the empire, especially ecclesiastical principalities, had ceased to exist. There had been personal unions of states for better defence, and personal union had been converted by Poland and Great Britain into organic union. Every one of these changes brought nearer the system under which the state was the common organization of all the people living in the same region, a possession which they were able to maintain because they had other things in common besides this machinery for police and defence and taxation. Their common feelings of feudal, military, dynastic, or merely official loyalty melted into common devotion to religious beliefs, or customs and ways of life. In some of the strongest states, as amongst the English, French, and Dutch, although there were minorities who spoke different languages, a dominant language was one of the binding links.

Thus the state and the nation each grew in strength and consciousness, or rather each was made stronger and more aware of itself by its own action and that of the other. A great part of the activity of statesmen was directed to bringing recalcitrant elements under control: we have seen it in their dealings with churches, armies, universities, feudal jurisdictions, and foreign infringements of their sovereignty. We have seen in their economic policy how the community came more thoroughly under control as it became more truly a community, and this was so not only in economic affairs but in every activity. In the seventeenth century there were places where governments deliberately degraded a language and its literature, as the Austrians did those of the Czechs, or encouraged them, as the French ministers did their own. On the other hand such measures of encouragement, in language and in everything else which tended towards national spirit, were not only imposed from above but welcomed and asked for from below. There were scholars and scientists who gloried in the official status of their academies, merchants who begged for higher tariffs, priests who were enthusiasts for the Gallican liberties. The rise of sovereignty was one aspect of the emergence of political communities which were also economic communities and communities of sentiment and civilization, some of them with a national groundwork.

The more liberal states, especially the Dutch republic and Great Britain, give us a warning that these developments were by no means everywhere alike, and we may draw another warning from the map of the baroque. It is true that the states were in some measure, and increasingly, the guardians of civilization. They had preserved the western way of life from the Turkish danger, and they had planted it over the world. It was their daily work to maintain the order and prosperity on which it always depended. But they were not its only guardians, and the communities which were forming under their auspices were not the only groupings on which civilization was based. Although the old European unity had been impaired, it still existed. Except for the changed relation to Russia, the state-system still kept its boundaries, and the common consciousness of similarity among Europeans and difference from the other continents grew stronger as these came to be better known. It was not, however, as definite as national feeling, and it was not maturing so rapidly. But there were other unities which transcended the frontiers of the states. The unity of the Catholic Church which the baroque reflected, was different in quality from the Christian unity of the Middle Ages. It was disciplined by the constant presence of danger. Although the circumstances of different countries, and especially the different relations of states to Catholicism, gave various colourings to Catholic thought and practice, they were more uniform than they had been, and perhaps less tinged by nationality. On the Protestant side few of the many churches and sects had much communication across national frontiers, and even the Calvinists never succeeded in bringing together an assembly representing all their members dispersed among the nations; but, as we have seen, there was some common Protestant consciousness and it contained much more than opposition to Rome.

The baroque also showed that the course of the arts might run contrary to that of political affairs. Usually the power of the state, the wealth of the community, and the brilliance of literature and the arts all rose and sank together. We have seen that this was so in Spain, France, England, and the Netherlands. If we cannot say exactly this about the Italian Renaissance, at least we can bring it under the wider statement that civilization was most alive when political life was not languid or uneventful but lively. Some of the most extravagant successes of the baroque, however, belonged to countries which were politically unsuccessful or declining, as were Spain and Portugal and Poland. They were commissioned by noblemen or ecclesiastics whose wealth and consequence were not affected by the miscarriages of the states; indeed baroque magnificence, with its disregard of structure and function, seems specially appropriate to an aristocracy which has no intimate contact with the other orders of society. In the seventeenth century there were countries where the aristocracies grew prouder and stronger; and, even where they were depressed by the rising monarchies, there was a growing separation between the aristocratic life and the life about it. Something of this kind happened even in the liberal and commercial countries. Dutch art in the middle of the century was patronized and appreciated by farmers and shopkeepers, as well as by the rich; but, for whatever reason, this ceased to be so at the time when French influence reached its height. In Holland, as in England, the scale and expense of life in great houses seems to have risen. Not only the scientific movement, but the Renaissance before it, deepened the division between cultivated minorities and the people in general. Popular art became more separate from the refined and expensive arts which served the powerful and the rich. The artist became more distinct from the craftsman, and, with his wider view of the arts of many places and periods, he became cosmopolitan, like the scientists.

Everywhere, however, there were still healthy popular arts, and modern collectors hunt for objects which were made in those days for the everyday use of ordinary people, not only because time has made them rarities, but for their beauty. Changes in transport had done little to free those who built small dwelling-houses from their dependence on local materials, and so long as the craftsman grew up in a tradition of working on stone or wood, or using colours, which belonged to his own immediate environment, he kept his creative vitality. And this popular art, none the less a part of European civilization for being local, had its parallels in industrial skill, in traditional religion and morality, and in proverbial wisdom, even if they shaded off into superstition and conservative obstinacy.

During the centuries which we have been surveying, popular civilization had not been stationary. The whole face of Europe had been altered by the economic changes and the political conflicts, which affected men in their masses, and by the articulate movements of ideas, which had worked upon these masses, for the most part, by teaching or example from above. In this brief outline it has been necessary to follow the thoughts and acts of the leaders, just as it may be necessary, in a brief history of a campaign, to trace the decisions of the commanders, but to omit the movements of companies or battalions or perhaps even of divisions. We should have mistold the history of these centuries if we had laid more stress on the preparatory steps which eventually resulted in universal education, manhood suffrage, or democracy in any of its forms. There had been more actual progress towards these than there had been towards a definitive map of Europe or the peaceful settlement of international disputes; but it was progress in preparing the conditions for them, intentionally or unintentionally, and not in bringing them into operation in institutions or even in making men's minds look forward to them. We break off in the early eighteenth century at a point where civilization was still thought of, almost universally, not indeed as existing for the sole benefit of the few, but as upheld by exceptional men whose rank or abilities made them responsible for it, and there was truth in this view. Nevertheless, it was also true that the rulers and leaders could not have done their work unless the peoples had responded to them: there can be no leaders unless they are followed. Some of the changes penetrated more and others less deeply into the compacted whole of society. A thousand men were influenced by Luther for every one who appreciated Rembrandt. There was endless violence, corruption, ignorance, ugliness, waste, and misery; but there was a civilization, marvellously rich and fertile, and it was sustained by society as a whole.

Note on Further Reading

FOR MANY YEARS the standard English work on the subjects of this book has been *The Cambridge Modern History*, which was completed in 1912. A *New Cambridge Modern History*, with twelve volumes of text, is in course of publication. The bibliographies in the earlier series are very full, but they contain little explanatory comment and are now out of date. The best way to find the titles of the modern authorities on any historical subject is to consult the appropriate article in the most recent edition of a good encyclopaedia. Similar information may be found in the four volumes of the *Subject-Index of the London Library* (published in 1909, 1923, 1938, and 1955) which are available in many libraries.

Readers who read for pleasure or for general interest, and who are not specially concerned to know what are the latest conclusions of scholars will, none the less, find it useful to learn something about the books they read in addition to what is contained within their covers. A book may have repellent faults and yet may give the best expression to valuable truths. Another book may be admirable in many ways and yet may have some misleading bias, or may be partly based on unreliable sources, or may have become obsolete in the light of subsequent discoveries. A reader who is forewarned of pitfalls like these will be able to allow for them and so will not be misled. If it is a new book it will probably have been reviewed in the *English Historical Review*, which began in 1886, or in the *American Historical Review*. If it is an older book written by a British author, an estimate of his standing as an historian can probably be found in the article on his life in the *Dictionary of National Biography*. Other countries have similar works of reference in their own languages. Many of the great historians are characterized and discussed in G. P. Gooch, *History and Historians in the Nineteenth Century* (2nd edition, 1952).

Index

Dates of monarchs are those of the years during which they reigned; of other persons are those of birth and death.